Healthy Church

Ten Spiritual Practices for Healthy Believers and Churches

Craig Tackett

Renown Publishing

Healthy Church / Craig Tackett
ISBN-13: 978-1-952602-26-9

To my friends and family at NBC On Main. Thank you for doing "messy" and "yummy" alongside me. Thank you for joining me in the struggle to become healthy followers of Jesus. Thank you for loving me on this journey towards being a healthy church. I am forever grateful to be your pastor.

CONTENTS

Why Health?

When we talk about being healthy, a lot of images spring to mind. Right off the bat, I think of nutrition and exercise and other ways to maintain good health. You might picture a hospital or a doctor's office or another place where we go when something with our health is not right. Or your mind might go right to thinking of what happens when a person's health is in dire straits and needs chemotherapy or emergency heart surgery.

And that's just physical health! When you add in emotional, mental, spiritual, and financial health, we start realizing that being healthy is a monumental task. There are so many things that can go wrong, whether it's because of something we do or something that happens to us.

I think it is interesting to note that the Bible refers to the church as a *body* of believers. In 1 Corinthians 12, Paul talks about how each person in the church is like a single body part, working together with other parts to create a single unit. Both Colossians 1:18 and Ephesians 5:23

describe Jesus Christ as the head of the body, with the understanding that the body is the church.

Now, it hurts my heart to say this, but I've seen many churches where the members don't look anything like a single body working together in community. It's more of an "I want what is mine," rather selfish mentality. Being a healthy body of believers takes work, commitment, and discipline—three things that, sadly, modern American Christians don't value as highly as they should.

I would like to paint a picture for you. Imagine a young man—we'll call him Tony—joins the army. Tony starts off incredibly well. He breezes through basic training and heads off to his assigned duties. But over time, Tony begins to slack off on his exercising. He begins to allow some junk food into his diet. He starts to drink here and there on the weekends. That drinking increases when he witnesses terrible things during a deployment. He doesn't get counseling, continues to spiral, and turns to gambling and pornography to help him escape his feelings.

How effective is Tony as a soldier now? Not only is he going to fail the physical tests of army life, he's also completely unprepared emotionally for the next difficult situation he might face.

Now, if Tony is the only soldier like this, his unit will likely get along just fine. But what if this sort of lifestyle becomes the norm among the people in his unit? What if most of the soldiers in Tony's squadron are equally unhealthy? They will not be able to protect themselves in combat. Their individual decisions may now put the unit, the mission, or even the war they are fighting together at risk.

It might seem a bit dramatic, but that's what's at risk when Christians ignore their spiritual health. A single unhealthy Christian might mostly do damage to himself, but if a church is made up largely of such unhealthy people, then the mission of the Kingdom is at risk. People who need to be told about the gospel aren't hearing it. We create converts, but no one is working to create or become disciples. That means there are negative, eternal consequences for some people surrounding these Christians.

That's not something we can take lightly.

So, why should you read this book? Why is the pursuit of spiritual health important? All living things tend to entropy, and if we're not pursuing health, we'll fall into disorder and sickness. If we're not pursuing a functional life, we'll fall into dysfunction. If we're not being successful—well, then we're unsuccessful. We become what we actively pursue. Just as a garden must be tended, or it returns to wilderness, we must be intentional in seeking growth and health.

In this book, we're going to focus on ten healthy practices that every believer and every church body needs to incorporate in order to stay on track with God's plan. Many of the practices must be carried out by individuals and also by the church as a whole. However, they are all grounded in the Scriptures and are vital for creating and sustaining healthy churches.

Let's be honest: growing healthier spiritually isn't easy. Just like it's difficult to start a new exercise program or change your eating habits, developing good spiritual discipline takes work. In order to help you process what you're reading and think through what changes you might need to make, I've included a workbook section at the end of each chapter. Please use these questions and the space provided to journal, pray, or dig in deeper with your small group.

There are many people who are truly hungry for God. Some readers will pick up this book with a heart that is ready to be fed. If that's you, I hope that when you are challenged, you meet it head on and take steps to grow as you "work out your salvation with fear and trembling" (Philippians 2:12). I pray that the words in these pages will be filled with the Spirit and that you will be moved by what you discover here. I hope that these truths take root in your life and in the life of your church family— and that they spark Kingdom changes in the world we're living in.

PROLOGUE

The Church

This book is about our health. It's about our spiritual wellness as it relates to being a part of a church family and as an individual believer in Christ. Since we're going to talk a lot about churches, let me pause and give you a quick definition for what a *church* should be.

Have you ever stopped and asked yourself, "What does it take to be considered a church?" I suspect most of us have visited or even been members of churches that seem to be little more than social clubs that meet in a building called a "church." But being a church has nothing to do with a building, the staff employed there, or the denomination to which they belong.

According to the Scriptures, there are only two things it takes to be considered a church. The first is righteous teaching of the Word. The second is that the ordinances of God are rightly celebrated. What does that mean? Let me delve briefly into both ideas.

It's very important that we emphasize the word *righteous* when we talk about teaching God's Word. If you've been around church long enough, I'm sure you've experienced a misuse of the Scriptures to fit almost any agenda. Righteous teaching is scripturally proper in both its context and application.

There are pastors who like to use the pulpit as an excuse to push a political or social agenda. There are even pastors who teach things that are in direct opposition to what the Bible says.

Now, we can all make mistakes. No one gets it right every time, so I certainly encourage you to extend grace when someone gets something wrong. I will not always get it right, and I certainly hope that my church family extends me grace when I fail in this area. However, if a church leader is spending time with God and allowing himself or herself to be instructed by the Bible, the Holy Spirit, and biblical scholars, righteous teaching should take place regularly.

Not only should righteous teaching happen, but the teaching of the Scriptures should also be the standard. It is fine to speak of finances when preaching, because Jesus did. It is fine to speak on sexuality in sermons; Jesus did that, too. But, when our messages become all about money, sex, family, politics, etc.—and the sermons become more about the topics than the Scripture—we have a problem. Teachers of the Word shouldn't start with an agenda and then find a Scripture to drop in as an afterthought to back it up. We must always begin with the Scriptures and trust the Holy Spirit to help us make the application to our lives.

What is your home church like? What feels comfortable to you when you seek a place of worship? Whether you prefer traditional organ music and a choir in matching robes or contemporary music and a pastor with a beard and man-bun, righteous teaching must be a part of your church experience. You should walk away feeling challenged and see a consistent pattern of spiritual growth.

Secondly, a church needs to practice the two ordinances outlined in the New Testament: baptism and communion. There's been a lot of contention in churches and denominations through the years about how these things must be carried out. I'm not going to take the time to dive into that here. Just know that these two things need to be happening in order for a group to call themselves a church.

These two ordinances are honorable celebrations of Christ's death and His glorious resurrection. When Jesus had the first communion with the disciples, He said to continue doing this "in remembrance of me" (Luke 22:19). Communion keeps our eyes on the cross, not on church politics or personal preference. Like a compass, it reorients our priorities to Christ.

And baptism is a vital reminder that our churches don't exist for our group of friends. The church exists to spread the gospel, to bring nonbelievers into God's kingdom. Baptism is a celebration of the forgiveness of our sins and the welcoming of new believers into the body. It's the initial testimony of our belief in the risen Savior. We celebrate the ordinances as a simple act of sincere obedience to Christ.

Am I? Are We?

The spiritual practices outlined in the following chapters must be done on two levels. Individual members of the church must engage in them in their own personal lives. And as a whole, the church must also carry out these practices corporately.

As you read this book, please ask yourself *"Am I?"* Are you doing each of these things in your personal walk with God? But you also need to ask, *"Are we?"* Is the body of believers you're a part of also walking in these practices?

Absence of any of the spiritual practices can be an indicator of poor health. This might be an individual problem or a bigger church-wide problem. Each practice is to be done by the "members" *and* by the "body". Consider the practice of tithing. It's certainly something individual Christians should do, but it's also something the local church should do. As a church body, if we're to be healthy, we need to give away a tithe of our income to Kingdom causes that aren't directly related to our home church.

We all have a responsibility both to ourselves and to our churches to be spiritually healthy. You can't replace a steel link in a chain with a paperclip and expect to haul a trailer. Each link must be strong in order for the chain to do its job.

It might be tempting to take up jogging and then decide you can eat whatever you want since you're exercising. We know that's not going to make for a healthy individual. Just the same, if your entire exercise class goes out for pizza and sodas after class? That's going to be one unhealthy group of people! It is important that we don't pick and choose which practices we want to be a part of and which ones we don't. They are all important and doing one and not the others may not help much.

As you read this book, you're going to find some practices might come easier for you than others. We all have preferences and skill sets. One person might find corporate worship a delight while another finds it monotonous or boring. For some, confessing sin might be easy but living responsibly is much more difficult for them.

Please don't dismiss a spiritual practice as unimportant simply because it isn't easy for you to follow. As much as anything, a healthy spiritual practice is a *discipline*, and this suggests that it will take work and require you to put aside your preferences and put in the effort it takes to succeed. If we are not challenged, we won't grow. If we're not growing, we're not really living the full and abundant life God has called us to.

I want you to be challenged to become a healthy member of a healthy church. So take the time to ask yourself, *"Am I?" "Are we?"*

CHAPTER ONE

Savoring Scripture

Your word is a lamp for my feet, a light on my path. I have taken an oath and confirmed it, that I will follow your righteous laws.

—Psalm 119:105–106

A healthy church is made up of individuals who believe the Scriptures are totally sufficient as an authoritative guide to the Christian life.

We've all done it. We buy a new microwave, drive home, and open the box. After wrestling the microwave out and discarding the protective Styrofoam, we put it on the counter and plug it in. We throw the instruction manual into the junk drawer, box up the extraneous paper, plastic, and cardboard and take it out to the trash.

When it comes time to use the new microwave we rarely, if ever, take the time to read the step-by-step instructions. I mean, it's a microwave. They're pretty easy to use, right? And most of the time, after some trial and error, we can get by just fine.

Now, you might never learn to use the special features. You may even have no earthly idea how many legitimately cool functions your new machine is capable of. It might be years later before you figure out what *that* button actually does. And when it comes time to do something tricky, like defrosting meat, we might (slim chance) dig out the manual and read that one particular section just to find out how long to defrost without partially cooking our chicken.

But no one is ever excited about reading the manual. You don't drive home from work thinking, "Gosh, I can't wait to get home and read the next section in my instruction booklet! I wonder what I'll learn from the old Owner's Manual tonight!"

Unfortunately, that's how we often treat the Bible. In fact, we have a lot of very unhealthy ideas about the Bible. It's not just a map. It's not just a list of rules and regulations. It is not merely an instruction manual. It is *alive*! But treating the Scriptures this way is not a new problem. After all, Jesus consistently rebuked the Pharisees for learning all of God's laws (rules and regulations) and totally ignoring God's character (The person of Jesus Christ). It's easy to treat the Bible like a map we only use if we've lost our way.

But the Bible isn't a last resort. It's not just a pill we swallow when we need it. It's so much more than a list of rules designed to ruin all your fun. However, the Bible *is* the eternal story of how a loving Creator redeemed His creation. It is the epic masterpiece of an everlasting Savior guiding His beloved Creation through the fall, salvation, and reconciliation. It's the story of how we can live the abundant life we were created for.

Healthy Christians make the Scriptures a vital part of their daily walk with God. Healthy churches spend time corporately and consistently digging into God's Word. They genuinely crave it. "As the deer pants for streams of water, so my soul pants [longs] for you" (Psalm 42:1). It is the nourishment our spirits need and without it, we aren't really following God at all; we're actually following our idea of who we think God should be.

The Scriptures Are Sufficient

There is a really important idea that I need you to understand: the Bible is *sufficient*, but it is not *exhaustive*. Let me say that again for the people in the back. You heard me correctly, the Bible is sufficient, but it is not exhaustive. The Bible is "living and active" (Hebrews 4:12 ESV). It is absolutely useful for teaching, rebuking, correcting, and training us (2 Timothy 3:16). It's a lamp for our feet and a light for our path (Psalm 119:105), and we are to treasure it in our hearts so that we don't sin (Psalm 119:11 NASB). The Bible is our authority. It gives us the laws and principles we need to live life God's way. But it doesn't spell out every answer to every problem we face in life.

Let me give you an example. In 1 Timothy 2:9, Paul gave instructions on how women should dress and act in church. He listed things like modest clothing, not having elaborate hairstyles, or not wearing pearls. If we take those words at face value, it would be sinful for a woman to wear a pearl necklace in church and that certainly isn't the way we live today.

The problem is, we can't make it about the pearls, the gold, or the hair. The minute we do, we trivialize the issue and miss the deeper understanding of why Paul wrote it and what the real issue was. You see, women in Timothy's church were focusing too much on what they wore and not enough on Jesus. They weren't coming in humble worship; they were parading in and showing off for everyone else. Their hearts were proud and self-centered.

Also, they became a distraction. When you are drawing the attention from God to yourself while others are in worship, therein lies the problem. It wasn't a pearl issue, it was a heart issue. It wasn't a gold issue, it was a modesty issue. The real issue is who is the center of attention during a worship experience. How do we keep our hearts and our eyes focused on God. Today, that Scripture might refer to low-cut blouses and miniskirts. But again, it is not a clothing issue. It's a matter of the heart.

There will be situations in your life where you can't find an explicit answer in the Bible. However, the more we study Scripture, the better we understand God's character, which often informs us of what is the right thing to do.

Is smoking wrong? How about dancing? Cheesecake? What about cohabitating? Is there a verse for that? Whether it's smoking, drinking, or that extra slice of cheesecake, we must consider the overall principles of Scripture in our decision making. But isn't that a difficult process?

Absolutely. So, as we look towards finding the answers in the Scriptures, consider the following. There are many very wise teachers and preachers who have come before us. It's a good practice to go and read their interpretations of the Scriptures. Listen to podcasts to help you better understand the Bible. Read books written by wise Christians. In Hebrews 12:1, it says we are "surrounded by such a great cloud of witnesses." Take advantage of the wisdom of those who have gone before us. Yet, always come back to God's Word and make sure that what these teachers are saying lines up with what God says.

We Need the Holy Spirit

This is where the rubber meets the road. Anytime we want to study, digest, teach, or interpret the messages in God's Word—we need to Holy Spirit! When a nonbeliever attempts reading the Bible, he or she might absorb the words, but they will likely miss out on the deeper meaning. Why? Well, because the Word of God tells us that "the natural man does not receive the things of the Spirit of God, for they are foolishness to him; nor can he know them, because they are spiritually discerned" (1 Corinthians 2:14 NKJV). We need the Holy Spirit to help us interpret God's Word!

Think about it like this: if you go to a 3D movie and don't put on the glasses, you can still understand what's going on, right? You can hear the words, figure out the plot, and generally get an understanding of what is going on. But without the glasses, you're missing the movie as it was created to be. You can't see the film and all of the nuances the director and producer worked so hard to create. The Holy Spirit is a lot like those 3D glasses when it comes to studying the Scriptures. Without Him, it's just not possible to read, understand, and carry out the Scriptures in the amazing way God intended them.

This is especially important because the Bible is never changing, but ever changing. What I mean is this: God will never change His character or His requirements of us and the Bible isn't ever going to be re-written or altered. However, culture changes. Society does get altered. People deal with things in different ways across the expanse of time and history. And, thanks to the Holy Spirit, the Bible addresses these things over all the centuries and in every culture. God's Word is always relevant.

Let's put that into context. Let's look again at what Paul said in 1 Timothy 2:9. Women are to dress modestly. The definition of *modest dress* changes from culture to culture and across the years, doesn't it? In India, women wear saris to church. Saris reveal part of the abdomen, yet this is not considered immodest in the least. In fact, these women use the ends of their saris to cover their heads during prayer, living out 1 Corinthians 11:5. In modern America, we would find it very immodest for a woman to come to church with part of her abdomen showing and we have no problem if women pray with their heads uncovered. By comparison, one hundred years ago, every woman wore a hat and gloves to church, and what women wear today would have been considered scandalous!

Is any of this sinful? Well, with the help of the Holy Spirit, wise teachers, and an understanding of God's character, we can get to the heart of the issue. It's not *really* about the covering or not covering of the head at all. It is all about approaching God with humility. When we pridefully rebel against authority, that is sinful. If a woman disregards the struggle of her brothers in Christ and dresses in a way that makes it difficult for the men around her to focus on God, that's a sin issue. In the same way if a man declares that all the lust he feels is due to women—and declares that men have no responsibility in the matter—so they must cover themselves from head to toe, that's also sinful. We must allow the Holy Spirit to inform our understanding of the Scripture.

How do we go about involving the Holy Spirit? I suggest that you begin by inviting Him to meet with you when you sit with your Bible. Ask for wisdom and guidance. When you come to a perplexing Scripture, pray for understanding. Don't just run your eyes over the page and then put your Bible on the shelf. Rather, ask the Spirit of God to reveal nuggets of truth to you along the way that you can apply to your daily life.

Savoring Scripture

It is imperative that we do more than simply read the Bible and memorize a bunch of verses. Memorization is important, but it's the application of the verses that matters most. The Pharisees would actually commit to memory entire books of the Bible, yet in many cases their lives were never changed. They would even tithe on their spices, but failed to realize that God called them to have generous hearts (Matthew 23:23). Do you see the difference?

Healthy believers savor God's Word. They genuinely crave it. They don't just chew and swallow, they let the flavor roll around in their mouths and appreciate the herbs, the char, the texture. They look forward to going back and having a second helping. We need to understand that the Scriptures are vital, and we should genuinely delight in them, rejoice in God's correction, and make them a central part of our lives.

Jesus told a parable about a farmer spreading seed. He explained that the seed is the Word of God (Mark 4:14). The seeds landed in different kinds of soil. Most of the seeds never took root. Only those seeds which landed in fertile soil grew into healthy plants. We must go to the Bible having prepared our hearts to take in what God has for us and we must let the Holy Spirit do His job of turning the seeds into strong plants with firm roots that bear much fruit.

Chapter One Questions

Am I? In what ways are you building your life on Scripture as your sufficient guide? Do you ask the Holy Spirit to prepare your heart and help you understand His Word? How are you savoring Scripture and applying it to your life?

_____

_____

_____

_____

_____

_____

_____

_____

_____

Are We? In what ways does your church exalt Scripture in your worship? Through preaching? How does or how can your church body keep each other accountable for both learning the Word and living the Word?

_____

_____

_____

_____

_____

_____

_____

_____

_____

_____

_____

_____

Journal: *The Bible is sufficient, but it is not exhaustive.* How can an individual or a church find biblically sound answers for questions that are not explicitly addressed in the Scriptures? What are some of the dangers that can come from either viewing the Bible as culturally irrelevant or from trying to make it give specific answers to questions it never addresses?

_____

_____

_____

_____

_____

_____

_____

_____

_____

_____

_____

_____

Action: Make a list, with coordinating verses, of the many ways that the Bible describes itself, such as a sword, light, food, etc. What do each of these word pictures say about how you should approach God's Word and how it can change your life?

Chapter One Notes

_____

_____

_____

_____

_____

_____

_____

_____

_____

_____

_____

_____

_____

_____

_____

_____

_____

_____

_____

_____

_____

CHAPTER TWO

Pursuing Jesus

What I mean is this: One of you says, "I follow Paul"; another, "I follow Apollos"; another, "I follow Cephas"; still another, "I follow Christ." Is Christ divided? Was Paul crucified for you? Were you baptized in the name of Paul?
—1 Corinthians 1:12–13

A healthy church is made up of individuals who pursue Jesus as the ultimate treasure.

A young couple gets married. We'll call them John and Mary. As most young couples do, they begin their married life with great enthusiasm. When John gets offered his dream job, Mary is very supportive.

But as time goes by, John starts spending more and more hours at work. He stops arriving home in time to eat supper with Mary and eventually only arrives home after she's already in bed. Any time they talk about his job, they walk away frustrated. After all, this job is his dream! The money is excellent. The co-workers are fantastic.

Over time, John can tell that something's not right in his marriage. Mary is distant and has a life of her own. The once-happy couple are now little more than roommates. And John has no idea how to fix the problem. It's not like he's pursuing something sinful. Work is valid, even biblical! But the pair are miserable.

So often, this is a picture of what happens in our marriages *and* in our churches. We start off with the best of intentions, eyes fixed firmly on Jesus. Yet, as the worship improves or the pastor brings in a bigger crowd, or the Children's ministry begins to boom, it's easy to slowly stop pursuing Jesus and start pursuing other things.

A healthy church pursues Jesus and Jesus alone. Not a pastor, not a style, not a building, and not a ministry—just Jesus.

What Are You Chasing?

We know that the Bible is our ultimate authority and that it is completely sufficient. It tells us that the ultimate treasure is the pursuit of Jesus Christ. In Philippians 3:7, Paul wrote, "But whatever were gains to me I now consider loss for the sake of Christ." Nothing else matters other than Jesus.

I grew up in a small-town church that had very traditional worship. When I went to college, I fell in love with contemporary praise and worship music. I learned that there were entire movements that garnered thousands of fans who came and built churches around these worship leaders. Over time, these churches faltered when the musician moved on to other projects. In fact, some churches closed because they were built on the incredible worship rather than Jesus.

When a church is entirely built upon a single person or group of people, it is destined to fail because man is fallible. Only Jesus is infallible. He is the solid rock that we need for our foundation. Basing our faith in a human's ministry is dangerous.

How many times have we seen churches rocked by scandal? The lead pastor is caught in his sin, or the music minister decides he doesn't want to follow Jesus anymore. And while these are big issues that should be of concern, a church that is pursuing Jesus will be able to continue pursuing Jesus even if their leader moves on. When the members of a church only come because they like this pastor's preaching style, they aren't going to stick things out for long. They are pursuing their own preferences and not Jesus.

It's like running a marathon. If you're running in a big group and someone takes the wrong turn, the whole group might follow that person. And while they're still running, they aren't going to reach their goal because they have veered off course.

Failing to pursue Jesus happens both at the individual level and at the corporate level. We must, as individuals, examine our hearts. Am I pursuing Jesus in my personal life? Am I more devoted to a particular worship leader or author? If I no longer had access to this person's work, would I still be chasing after Jesus?

And we need to examine our churches as a whole. Are we as a congregation pursuing Jesus? Is our worship truly pointing to Jesus or is it all about the euphoria of singing together as a group? Is our pastor helping us to stay rooted in the Scriptures and engaging with the Holy Spirit? How much is the sin of pride impacting our leadership? These are difficult but healthy questions to ask.

Good Things Versus God Things

What makes this whole thing confusing is the fact that most of these are good things. Worship music is good! Preaching is good! Growing the church is good! They are all important parts of a healthy, vibrant church. So, how can we look at them and say that they are problematic?

Let's take a moment to look at Jesus' temptation in the wilderness to give us some understanding. Matthew chapter 4 tells us the story.

Before Jesus started His ministry, He spent forty days in the wilderness (Matthew 4). At the end of the forty days, Satan himself came to tempt the Son of God. The very first thing Satan did was try to get Jesus to turn stones into bread so that He could eat.

I think this illustrates my point. After forty days of fasting, Jesus was hungry (Matthew 4:2). Yeah, no kidding. Satan came along and told Jesus to turn stones into bread and eat. On the surface, that doesn't seem like a big deal. So what? Jesus was hungry, shouldn't He eat?

But the Bible tells us that for Jesus in this circumstance, it would have been sinful. Jesus said, "It is written: 'Man shall not live on bread alone, but on every word that comes from the mouth of God'" (Matthew 4:4). Jesus Himself had his eyes focused on God. God had commanded His Son to fast, and Jesus took that very seriously.

The same thing occurs immediately after. Satan took Jesus to the top of the temple. He tried to get Jesus to jump off the top and fall toward the ground knowing that the angels would catch Him, and He would surely not die. What's the problem here? I mean He is the Son of God. The temple courts would have been a busy place. This could have revealed God's power and authority. That's good right? But Jesus replied that "we are not to tempt God." God has a plan, a plan that is never changing and ultimately good. We should not attempt to alter that plan for our gain. The point is, good things aren't always God things.

We can spend so much time striving to do good things that we miss God altogether. Jesus is our treasure and if we stop treating Him that way, we have let something else become the thing we worship. Whether it's a new building, a huge congregation, or innovative ideas, if something other than Jesus becomes our primary aim, we have a problem.

Just ask Martha. In Luke 10:38–42, Jesus showed up to have dinner at the home of Mary and Martha. Martha felt the need to "host" Jesus and worked in her home to present an environment of hospitality, which she was gifted to do. She baked, roasted, mixed, and worked hard to please Jesus with a meal and with her service to Him. When she came into the room upset because she was working herself into a frenzy and Mary was merely sitting listening to Jesus, He lovingly but sternly corrected her.

He essentially let her know that He did not ask for a buffet or a five-course meal or her hard work in the kitchen. He came to her house to be with her. She was so busy serving Jesus that she neglected to simply be with Him. Man, church, won't that preach? How many of us have gotten so caught up in serving Jesus—in kid's choirs, VBS, committee meetings, financial meetings, staff responsibilities—that we never actually sit with Him. Do you understand that what God wants is *you*? He really wants to be with you.

It is vastly more important to worship God than to listen to great worship music. It's more important to hear what God has to say than to follow a specific preacher. It's more important to have genuine relationships with nonbelievers than to have a church full of people who barely know Jesus. A place where people hop from congregation to congregation based on who gives them what they want or says the things they want to hear.

A healthy church has checks and balances in place to keep itself from letting idols grow in their people. A healthy church doesn't treasure the pastor or worship leader or the building. Those aren't hills to die on. They treasure Jesus and the pursuit of knowing Him more.

WORKBOOK

Chapter Two Questions

Am I? What are some good things (or people) other than Jesus that you have pursued in the name of Christianity? How has each fallen short or disappointed you? What things most often distract you from keeping your eyes on Jesus?

_____

_____

_____

_____

_____

_____

_____

_____

_____

Are We? Looking at the church globally, as well as the church in America, what are some "agendas" that you see churches pursuing instead of seeking Jesus? What about your own local church? Does a survey of your church's worship bulletin or newsletter show evidence that Jesus is the priority over programs, buildings, personalities, or trends?

_____

_____

_____

_____

_____

_____

_____

_____

_____

_____

_____

Journal: What are some good things that help you keep your focus on Jesus, and what are some good things that tend to become distractions from Jesus in your life? How can you, like Mary of Bethany (Luke 10:42), choose what is lasting and best?

_____

_____

_____

_____

_____

_____

_____

_____

_____

_____

_____

Action: Memorize Hebrews 12:1–2. In your small group at church, discuss hindrances and sins and how you can help each other to stay focused and to endure.

Chapter Two Notes

CHAPTER THREE

Practicing Ordinances

And [Jesus] took bread, gave thanks and broke it, and gave it to them, saying, "This is my body given for you; do this in remembrance of me."
—Luke 22:19

When the people heard this, they were cut to the heart and said to Peter and the other apostles, "Brothers, what shall we do?" Peter replied, "Repent and be baptized, every one of you, in the name of Jesus Christ for the forgiveness of your sins. And you will receive the gift of the Holy Spirit."
—Acts 2:37–38

A healthy church is made up of individuals who practice the ordinances assigned in Scripture.

People love to belong. Our hearts are warmed when we spot someone wearing a t-shirt from the college we attended or with a bumper sticker announcing they are fans of the same band. When one Jeep owner spots another, they wave to each other, even if they are strangers. Fans of the same sports teams have their own little rituals.

Why do we love to do these things? Do they really matter? Well, yes. They matter to us a great deal, and I think there are two reasons why. First, we love rituals that associate us with a certain group, because it tells the rest of the world that we're "in." We are true fans! We are alumni of this school! We support something special! And, secondly, rituals remind us that this is an important part of who we are. I worked my way through college and got my degree at this university, and I'm proud of it! I have great taste in music or books or hobbies or cars or sports or [fill in the blank]! It helps us feel like we belong.

There are times throughout a culture's history when rituals and traditions matter more and times when they matter less. Some generations value these things highly, and some disregard the old ways. Still, there are some things we may never disregard. No matter how much a person scoffs at tradition, he or she will probably eat turkey on Thanksgiving and think longingly of snow at Christmas. And, really, looking down on the way the previous generations did things doesn't stop us from choosing new traditions to value.

Practicing Ordinances

I already mentioned briefly a few simple things that it takes for a group of people gathering together to be a church. We know, of course, that a church is more than a building. In fact, in the early days of the church, most Christians met in people's homes. We didn't have paid clergy and buildings of worship throughout Europe for hundreds of years after Christ's death. So, what is the difference between a group of people gathering and talking about God occasionally, on one hand, and an actual church, on the other? Having a leader? The number of members? Registering with a denominational conference?

I believe that what makes a group a church is the righteous teaching of Scripture and the consistent practicing of two ordinances: baptism and communion. Jesus gave us a lot of instructions while He was on earth. For instance, we were told to love our neighbors as ourselves, pay our taxes, and forgive those who offend us. However, there are two specific things Jesus told His followers to do once they became followers of and believers in Him. Those things were—you guessed it—baptism (Matthew 3:12–17; Acts 2:38) and communion (Matthew 26:26–29; 1 Corinthians 11:17–32).

And over the centuries, these things have become sacred to Christians everywhere. They are practiced around the world and in many ways. No one else practices baptism and communion. They are only for people who claim that their trust is in Jesus.

Baptism

There has been a lot of dispute among Christians over how baptism must be done. I'm not going to argue that here. I have my beliefs about how it should be done, but I recognize that other people do it differently for a variety of reasons. We all have to stand before God and answer for ourselves, and if it bothers Him, I'll let Him deal with it. For now, I will choose to baptize in a way that honors what I understand Jesus' instructions to be. It is important, however, to understand why we should practice baptism.

First, we baptize because that was the example Jesus set for us. It is what He did, so it is what we should do. Jesus' baptism was a beautiful and symbolic moment. All of the people around at that time would have recognized the acknowledgement of who Jesus was through the testimony of John the Baptist and the voice of God saying, "This is my Son" (Matthew 3:16–17). That moment would have solidified Jesus' role in the minds of the people as a true rabbi and teacher.

I also think something tangible happens during baptism that is also vital to Christians. When we are baptized, we are making a public statement about where we put our trust. It is our first opportunity to give our testimony without saying a word. I believe baptism should, whenever possible, take place around other people. It absolutely does not have to, and it certainly doesn't make it more or less spiritual. But I believe that when believers are baptized, God uses their testimony to bring others to Him.

Baptism is an outward sign of an inward change. We are stating that we believe in Jesus, who died for our sins and rose again. Baptism should be the standard for all believers. It is the way we declare our belonging to the "team" of Christ-followers. We must humble ourselves by recognizing our sin, declaring that we are repentant and that we are choosing obedience to God.

And the reaction of the rest of the church should be applause and resounding praise! Baptism should be celebrated by the people in the church family with great joy.

The Lord's Supper

Once we give our lives to Jesus and know Him as our personal Lord and Savior, we may then participate in communion. I don't know about you, but when I was a kid, I sure didn't understand why communion mattered. It only meant that we would get snacks in church and the sermon would be shorter. It was a good day when we came in and saw the white cloth on the table in front of the pulpit.

But practicing the Lord's Supper is one of the most meaningful things we can do. It's a time to remember Jesus' sacrificial life and death. It's a chance to humbly examine our hearts, confess our sins, and begin the act of repentance. It's a place to wonder at the glory of God, who gave His Son to pay for our sins.

Again, churches practice communion in different ways. Some do this every week. Some do it once a month. Some have wine, some juice; some use bread, some crackers. Again, what matters is the humble remembrance and repentance.

For my church, I want us to have communion randomly and regularly. I want to celebrate the Lord's Supper often enough to remember but not so often that it becomes no more than a meaningless ritual. I can't control people's hearts—that's God's job—but I will do everything I can to help keep the Lord's Supper something that absolutely matters in the spiritual walk of the people I am called to lead.

Because, for people who have a personal relationship with Jesus Christ, we must take the time to examine our hearts and to remember His incredible sacrifice. We must never forget why we gather together and for whom we gather. Baptism says, "I choose You because You have chosen me." Communion says, "I remember." These things keep us focused on the One who matters in church.

We follow Christ's ordinances because we are told to and obedience should be the fruit of our love for Him. It's important to observe them *consistently* because they testify of, and remind us of, Christ's sacrifice for us and our new life in Him. These practices set apart Christian churches.

Jesus Christ died for our sins, and we in turn must die to ourselves and claim our new life in Christ. And we must remember what He did for us and not take it for granted, "For it is by grace you have been saved, through faith—and this is not from yourselves, it is the gift of God—not by works, so that no one can boast" (Ephesians 2:8–9). It is not anything we did; we are only saved because He gave His life for ours. And that is worth giving our lives for and remembering always.

Chapter Three Questions

Am I? Have you been baptized in a way that honors your understanding of the scriptural mandate? If not, what is hindering you from following Christ in this step of obedience? Are you honoring the ordinances by your attendance and participation when they are observed? When you participate in communion, are you merely going through the motions, or does it mean something to you? How can this be a tool to draw you closer to God?

_____

_____

_____

_____

_____

_____

_____

_____

_____

_____

_____

Are We? Does your church practice the ordinances of baptism and communion? How do these ordinances keep you drawing close to the heart of God as a community? What are some ways that a church can keep the celebration of the ordinances fresh through changing up the style, observing them in a different location, or giving more in-depth teaching regarding them?

_____

_____

_____

_____

_____

_____

_____

_____

_____

_____

_____

Journal: Examine your heart in preparation for the Lord's Supper, and follow up by writing down your thoughts of remembrance and praise after partaking in this ordinance.

_____

_____

_____

_____

_____

_____

_____

_____

_____

_____

_____

_____

Action: Study the Old Testament Passover and its parallels to modern-day communion. What insights does the Jewish Seder meal give regarding the Lord's Supper (which was instituted by Christ during Passover)?

Chapter Three Notes

CHAPTER FOUR

Chasing Holiness

You were taught, with regard to your former way of life, to put off your old self, which is being corrupted by its deceitful desires; to be made new in the attitude of your minds; and to put on the new self, created to be like God in true righteousness and holiness.
—Ephesians 4:22–24

A healthy church is made up of individuals who chase holiness by actively pursuing a godly life.

Christianity has a bad reputation. The truth of the matter is, we have brought it upon ourselves. Unbelievers picture us sitting at home doing boring things, checking off our "holier than thou" to-do lists and spending all our time finding new ways to look down on everyone else. It's likely that a lot of so-called Christians don't think much better of Christians in general, either. Hypocrisy is rampant. Church members seem to squabble consistently amongst themselves. Self-centeredness appears to be the order of the day in a lot of congregations. We often see an attitude of, "If it isn't going my way, fix it or else my family and I will leave." I really don't think it is supposed to be that way.

If you study the Word, you'll see that God has something else for us. He wants us to live on earth the way He originally planned. We'll spend time meeting with Him in the garden, worshiping Him, and building His kingdom together. Our time won't be sitting around doing nothing, nor will it be focused on our own personal happiness.

A lot of Christians hear that and groan. We wonder how we could ever be truly fulfilled living wholly for God. How much fun can that be? How can we spend eternity worshiping God? Will we have to serve each other all the time? That doesn't sound heavenly.

Such reservations concern me. You see, God's kingdom is a place where God is King. Where He is honored, loved, worshiped, and obeyed. And when Jesus was on earth, He even prayed, and taught us to pray, these words: "Thy kingdom come, Thy will be done in earth, as it is in heaven" (Matthew 6:10 KJV). His "will be done "*right now.* We're not just supposed to be living our lives however we want and giving God ten percent of our time and attention. We are supposed to be pursuing Him all the time. Yup, you read that right: *all the time.*

Determine Your Starting Point

Let me give this some context. What we are commanded to do, as in Ephesians 4:24, is to pursue holiness both for ourselves and for our churches. Holiness is being set apart for the cause of Christ. It's all about spending time and putting in the effort to do the things God wants for us in every situation. It's about being brokenhearted when we sin. And it's about working hard to be more like Christ.

Paul likened the disciplined life of a Christian to a runner's preparation for a race: "Do you not know that in a race all the runners run, but only one gets the prize? Run in such a way as to get the prize. Everyone who competes in the games goes into strict training. They do it to get a crown that will not last, but we do it to get a crown that will last forever" (1 Corinthians 9:24–25).

Consider an athlete who commits to running a marathon. There is a significant amount of planning, time, commitment, and discipline that goes into completing a marathon successfully. Running coach Greg McMillan says six key factors to a successful marathon are "stable mileage; long runs; grooving goal pace; leg durability; fueling; and mental toughness."[1] An athlete will not run a marathon well without intentional action before and during the race. And there are different types of marathon training plans for people who have varying levels of experience with running. The point is, you can't wake up one day, decide you're going to run a marathon that morning, and be successful.

Living a holy life in Christ is a daily grind. As Christians, we are in a marathon, and that marathon is a call to constantly and consistently grow in our walk with Christ. Healthy Christians do this joyfully. Not only do we recognize that we're sinners, but we also earnestly desire to be more like Christ. We're to delight when we get it right and mourn when we get it wrong. And all of this is done purely, out of a deep love for our Savior.

If that doesn't describe you, don't worry. You're not alone. Pursuing holiness is a lifelong process. It's difficult to look in the mirror, recognize your failings, and humbly ask for help. But it is a sign of maturity and health, and it's something we all need to be striving for.

So, what's the first step? It's examining yourself and determining where you currently are.

Imagine that you want to get to Disneyland. You type the coordinates into your GPS and then get frustrated when it doesn't tell you where to go. You see, it's one thing to know where you want to go, but it's another thing to know where you're starting point is. And, as the example with the GPS will tell you, you must know where you're starting from if you're going to get anywhere.

If you want to be tithing ten percent, you need to first look at where you are. Are you giving at all? No? Well, start giving what you can, and find ways to build up to that ten percent. It might take some time and some mistakes. If you want to spend an hour praying and reading your Bible, where are you starting? You spend five minutes a day listening to a podcast? Great, you can begin with that time block. Now, let's start working your way up to ten minutes of reading your Bible and maybe five minutes of praying.

Honestly assessing where you are spiritually is a crucial first step. It's the difference between someone who wants a relationship with God and someone who wants God to just do whatever they want. You see, it takes humility and hard work to pursue holiness. Not all of us want to examine our hearts and dig down to the root of our sin issues. And even fewer of us want to give up our sinful habits once we start seeing them for what they are.

The good news is that you don't have to get it right the first time. When a baby learns to walk, he falls down a lot. Well, consider yourself a baby Christian. You see where you want to be and start learning how to walk toward it. There are going to be times when you mess up, run to the Father, ask forgiveness, and get set back on your feet to try again. But you have to get up and get going. You must realize that you want to be over *there* and that you have to be intentional to make it happen.

Actively Pursue the Right Goals

A vital part of pursuing holiness is chasing the right goals. As human beings, we're really good at wanting the right things for the wrong reasons. We befriend the homeless man while secretly hoping someone is watching and thinking well of us. We long to be the best Christian so that God brings a spouse into our lives. We want to show up our sister-in-law or the guy who dumped us or our circle of church friends.

You know what? It may not be the most desirable motive to begin with, but God can work with that. He can transform our sinful desires into glorious ones that achieve His eternal plans. Don't let your fear of doing things for the wrong reasons keep you from ever starting. God is bigger than that. He can handle whatever comes. You just need to get started and keep assessing honestly, and God will help you to find the right goals for the right reasons. You should be most concerned about not moving forward at all. Christianity is not meant to be lived on a treadmill—going through the motions but getting nowhere. Stagnation is far more dangerous than stumbling your way forward.

Perhaps this situation found in nature will help you better understand the concept. What happens when a river or stream stops moving? When the water is not moving or flowing, it becomes stagnant. Stagnant water is dangerous. It doesn't take long for the chemical makeup of that water to change once it stops flowing. Soon it is not able to sustain life. Eventually, the water develops a stench or an odor. It attracts unfortunate bacteria and bugs. It is no longer life-sustaining and, in fact, is now life-threatening.

Sadly, a stagnant Christian and a stagnant church can produce the same results. If we are not consistently making an effort to move, learn, and grow, the results can be detrimental to us and those around us. The important thing is that your heart is set on consistently moving forward even if you make mistakes along the way.

Let's be honest, pursuing holiness is messy. It's hard to dig up all of the stuff we'd rather keep buried deep inside. I might finally be pursuing a good goal with pure motives, but that doesn't mean the guy next to me is doing as well. Feelings get hurt, we sin against each other, and we expose our most vulnerable selves. We need to talk about stuff we'd rather not. It's vital that the older generation be open about their struggles with things like pornography, racism, and gossip. We need to tell our young people what the lines are in a romantic physical relationship, not expect them to figure it out in the heat of the moment.

So, how do we reach the right goals? In Christian-speak, we say that we need to practice spiritual disciplines. There are hundreds of excellent resources out in the world, so I'm not going to reinvent the wheel here. People sometimes include different disciplines in their list, but let me hit on a few major ones that most everyone agrees on.

Spiritual discipline includes reading the Bible regularly and spending time talking to God about what we've read. It includes spending time daily in prayer, not only for ourselves but for those around us, too. It includes fasting from food for a period of time so we can learn how to say no to our bodies' desires in pursuit of holiness. It includes tithing. It includes confessing our sin and repenting of it. It includes bringing glory to God through acts of worship and praise, both corporately and individually.

Consider these disciplines the exercises your spiritual life needs to grow strong and healthy. Start small if any of them are new to you. There are so many great resources available through blogs and books and podcasts. Exercise these disciplines and you will find yourself moving toward your goal of holiness.

Chapter Four Questions

Am I? Is Christianity something you check off your to-do list, or does loving and following Christ permeate every single part of your life? Has the fear of failure caused you to fall into patterns of stagnation or a lack of forward motion? How can you see growth in holiness in your life, and where do you think are the areas that currently need the most growth? What ways can you move forward, even if messily?

_____

_____

_____

_____

_____

_____

_____

_____

_____

_____

_____

_____

Are We? What are some hard but honest conversations that relatively mature believers need to have with newer believers? How can the idea of mentoring or discipleship help younger or less-mature Christians grow into leaders who prioritize holiness and practice spiritual disciplines?

_____

_____

_____

_____

_____

_____

_____

_____

_____

_____

_____

Journal: _Honestly assessing where you are spiritually is a crucial first step._ How are you doing in practicing the various spiritual disciplines? How do you want to grow? Set three goals—one for your devotional life, one for outreach/giving, and one for a spiritual discipline—that you have never exercised before or have slacked off on doing.

_____

_____

_____

_____

_____

_____

_____

_____

_____

_____

_____

Action: Choose a book (or other resource) about spiritual disciplines and work through it with a small group at your church. Encourage each other in the practice of the disciplines and hold each other accountable to keep working at your goals.

Chapter Four Notes

_____

_____

_____

_____

_____

_____

_____

_____

_____

_____

_____

_____

_____

_____

_____

_____

_____

_____

_____

_____

_____

_____

CHAPTER FIVE

Responsible Freedom

I run in the path of your commandments, for you have set my heart free.
—Psalm 119:32 *(WEB)*

What then? Shall we sin because we are not under the law but under grace? By no means!
—Romans 6:15

A healthy church is filled with individuals who celebrate their freedom in Christ seriously and responsibly.

Sometimes it feels like we live in the most depraved and sinful era that has ever existed, but I'm not certain that is true. Since the fall in the garden of Eden (Genesis 3), sin has always been prevalent in every generation, in every life, and in every part of the world. The world got so evil that God literally had to flood it (Genesis 6–8). Sodom and Gomorrah were so incredibly depraved that

God had no choice but to wipe them out, so that the evil which consumed them didn't continue to spread (Genesis 19).

The world of the New Testament was equally filled with sinful practices. There were temples everywhere, with all kinds of things permitted in the worship of one god or another. Prostitution, homosexuality, gluttonous feasts, drunkenness, and the keeping of slaves were all a normal part of Roman society.

The early church had a lot to figure out. What was permissible? What wasn't? If we are saved and our sins forgiven, does it really matter whether or not we sin? I mean, Jesus wipes them all away. Paul and the other early church leaders had their work cut out for them in teaching the new Christians how the kingdom of God needed to operate here on earth. How do the mandates of Scripture intertwine with the cultural realities of life?

Christianity spread throughout the Roman empire into all corners of Europe. It moved through Asia and Africa. Missionaries went to the New World to reach the people there. America became a country and started to spread from the Atlantic to the Pacific.

And that's about where our ancestors came into the picture. They eagerly and passionately fought to establish churches and religious freedom all across this country. They lived in a different era and, in many ways, a different culture than the one that exists today. In order to set themselves apart from the unbelievers around them, to stand strong and avoid temptation, certain guidelines were adopted.

Think about towns in which the main source of

entertainment was a saloon with a brothel. To go into such a place meant you were most likely looking to get drunk, to gamble, or to hire a prostitute. For Christians in those days, the only dancing they ever saw might have been in such a place, and none of them would ever want to be seen as someone who would partake in those kinds of behaviors. And so, the culture of their church was one that didn't dance. Similarly, the only card playing that people did was gambling, so likewise, this became something that wasn't done in the church. Making the rule, "We don't play cards," was a way to help reformed gamblers not to fall into temptation.

Unfortunately, as time went by, these rules and guidelines became viewed as sin issues in every case. Any card playing was considered sinful, even if gambling wasn't involved. I remember believing that cards, dancing, tobacco, and alcohol were things the Bible specifically spoke out against.

During Prohibition, it was against the law to buy or sell alcohol. This was brought about by a strong group made up of many powerful men and women who believed in temperance, or abstaining from drinking alcohol. Temperance came from a good place. Mothers and children were often beaten by drunk fathers. Men wasted the rent money on alcohol. And so the temperance movement believed that if there was no alcohol, these problems would disappear.

Of course, they didn't. Temperance lost popularity when it didn't fix the problem, and soon it was again legal to buy and sell alcohol. So, is it okay for a Christian to drink alcohol or not? Can they dance? Or play poker?

In fact, how do we know whether or not all sorts of things are allowed? The Bible doesn't actually say, "Thou shalt not smoke," yet many believe it's not allowed. What about swearing? Getting a tattoo? Are we going to discuss pants and dresses? Short hair or long hair?

Legalism and License

A healthy Christian understands that he or she has to find the balance between responsibility and freedom. You don't want to err on the side of legalism, making an impossible list of rules to keep yourself from sinning. Neither do you want to brandish your "my sins are forgiven" license and do whatever you want.

Is dancing a sin? Not in and of itself. King David danced in the streets in celebration of what God had done for the Israelites as an act of unhindered worship (2 Samuel 6). Is drinking alcohol a sin? Not according to the Bible. Tobacco isn't even mentioned. In and of themselves, many things are not sinful. But we are really, really good at taking things that are innocent and allowing them to manifest as sin in our lives.

Jesus never said everyone should avoid alcohol. Read the Gospels and you'll see how silly it is to even suggest such a thing. At that time, nearly everyone drank wine. It was one of the only safe things to drink. People would no more avoid drinking wine than we'd avoid eating sandwiches. However, the problem is not alcohol itself; it's drunkenness.

If you are someone who struggles with addiction or has a history of alcoholism, choosing not to drink alcohol is the right decision. For you, drinking alcohol is an unhealthy choice because you know you can't stop with one drink. One drink will lead to another, and you will fall into sinful patterns.

Let me say this another way. For some of us, there are certain TV shows, movies, and video games that cause us to lust. They aren't strictly pornographic, but they sure get us heading in the wrong direction. If that's the case, it is unhealthy for us to watch those things. Is the show inherently sinful for all people? Maybe not, but if it is for me, I need to avoid it. It doesn't have to be on a big list of shows that no Christian anywhere can watch, but it needs to be on my personal list of movies that I avoid.

Finding Balance

A healthy Christian celebrates freedom in Christ while avoiding sin. We can pervert any good thing into a sinful thing without much effort. Case in point: I love to eat. I don't just like it—I love it! Cooking and sharing food and enjoying food is my escape. I believe God intended for us to enjoy all the things He created for us. I believe there are millions of combinations of foods, herbs, spices, acids, and more that resound the excellence of the Creator and are exactly why God told us to eat and to drink and to be joyful! Still, even food can become sinful. It has been taboo over the years to speak of these things, but food perverted is gluttony. Yes, gluttony. And in a nation where the leading cause of death is heart disease and the fourth leading cause is stroke[2]—both of which are obesity-related[3]—maybe it's time we take notice.

Pleasant talk between friends can be perverted into gossip. Healthy questioning of leaders can be perverted into open rebellion. And to be clear, sex was created by God. It is designed for our pleasure. It is a gift. But it can be, and has been, incredibly perverted across the expanse of history.

What's the answer? Do we avoid every potentially sinful thing? Should I only eat crackers and water so I don't become a glutton? Should we stay alone for fear of becoming a gossip? No, of course not! Should I only spend time with men so that I don't lust after women? Nope. This is where we begin to creep into legalism.

We must remember that we are called to do more than celebrate freedom; we are called to celebrate freedom in Christ. This world has many good things in it that are very enjoyable. Yet our purpose in life is not to make those things the center of our world. It's nice to be comfortable and do things you enjoy, but self-comfort is not to be your ultimate goal. It's nice to look good and have pretty things to wear, but your appearance is not to become the most important thing in your life. It's nice to be successful in your work, but that is not more important than serving God.

Setting Yourself Up for Success

Proverbs 3:5–6 is a familiar set of verses: "Trust in the LORD with all your heart and lean not on your own understanding; in all your ways submit to him, and he will make your paths straight." How do we figure out if we should do something or not? Go to God with it. Take the time to listen to the Lord and to search the Bible. Honestly examine your heart and your motives.

And let me say this: if you have to ask whether or not something is wrong, try not doing it at all. It's probably better to avoid a pitfall rather than fall in. Again, don't let yourself fall into legalism. Just because you lust when you go to the beach and see women in bikinis doesn't mean going to the beach is a sin for all Christians. If you find you can't resist temptation, avoid the situation. But if you are able, with the help of the Holy Spirit, to stay free from sin, then it's possible to carefully exercise that freedom. Filter every choice you make through two checks: Am I loving God? And am I loving people?

We must continually go to God. We must get in the habit of seeking Him out, of talking to wise people, and of checking our hearts. This is how we find the balance between legalism and license.

It is wise to address a phrase here that may or may not have jumped into your mind while reading this chapter. We have all heard the expression, "Everything in moderation." This chapter is about finding balance between declaring things to be sinful that are not sin and allowing things to happen that are sin. This begs the question, "Are we saying that everything in moderation is okay?" I'd like to quote Paul here and say, "By no means!" (Romans 6:2a).

I vehemently disagree with the suggestion that everything is okay in moderation. An adulterous relationship "on occasion" is not permissible. Allowing yourself to lie, as long as it is less than once a month, is not okay. If you only steal when completely necessary, it doesn't make it right. This phrase cannot and should not be our standard. The gospel, the person of Jesus, and the Holy Spirit must be our guide as we navigate this life together.

Support the Brothers

Let me give you one more filter: we need to evaluate if our actions will cause any of our brothers or sisters to stumble. First Corinthians 8:9 warns, "Be careful, however, that the exercise of your rights does not become a stumbling block to the weak."

I faced a situation in which two single girls, who were actively following Jesus, came to me and asked if it was wrong to move in with a single man from the church. They assured me there was nothing sinful taking place. He owned a house and was able to offer them affordable rent. But the girls wanted to know if this was okay from a biblical standpoint.

I told them I wanted to take some time to think and pray about it. I searched my Bible and didn't find anything that explicitly said not to do this. "Thou shalt not cohabitate" just wasn't anywhere to be found. It was possible, I knew, for the three of them to live together without sinning. Sure, it might be more of a temptation, but they also might be able to withstand any of that.

However, the Holy Spirit brought something to mind for me. This young man was involved in leadership with the youth group. It could be a real stumbling block for some of our young people if they saw him living with two women. The example he was going to set for them could be a benchmark for decision-making in their lives. These younger Christians might think, "If he can do it, it's fine for me," and jump into a situation in which they aren't able to stand up to temptation.

Now, it's not fair sometimes to have to make a decision in our lives based on the mere possibility that others may fail because of it. But this is how sacrifice works. This is what humility looks like, lived out in love for one another. It is what Paul meant by, "Do nothing from selfish ambition or vain conceit, but in humility consider others better than yourselves. Let each of you look not only to his own interests, but also to the interests of others" (Philippians 2:3 ESV).

Healthy Christians value other people's ability to resist sin above their own freedom. When we declare ourselves followers of Christ, we know our example, our words, and our habits will come under scrutiny and have the ability to affect His body as a whole. It would be detrimental to ask a recovering alcoholic to meet me at a bar for a Bible study. Taking a brother who struggles with lust to certain movies would be irresponsible.

I have the freedom to do many things, but I also have a responsibility to Christians around me who are weaker in certain areas. Now, that doesn't mean I should take their sin issue and make it the basis for a rule for myself. Rather, out of deference to this person, I will avoid this activity in this person's presence but be honest about the fact that I participate in it elsewhere.

Think about this in terms of parents and children. There are a lot of things we adults say and do that we don't say or do around our kids. We might also eat certain vegetables around our kids that we wouldn't often prefer or choose so that they learn to eat them also. I am absolutely not endorsing "radar detector" Christianity by saying it's okay to sin as long as you don't get caught. However, we are responsible for our children, and we want to set an example for them. In the same way, there are Christians who are in the early stages of their walk, and we need to set examples for them in the same way.

Healthy Christians who live in the freedom of Christ yearn not only to be obedient to God but also to live in a way that leads others there, too. Immature Christians demand their freedom. Mature Christians graciously sacrifice their freedom in order to help others. It's a delicate balance, but a beautiful symphony when the Holy Spirit guides us to unhindered freedom in Christ.

Chapter Five Questions

Am I? What are some areas about which the Bible doesn't speak specifically that have been issues in your life or have led you into sin? Did you seek God's will before making decisions regarding these issues? If so, how did He guide you? If not, do you regret the decisions you made? What are some filters you can use when deciding if you should engage in actions that aren't explicitly addressed in the Bible?

_____

_____

_____

_____

_____

_____

_____

_____

_____

_____

_____

Are We? How can a church remain sensitive to its weaker brothers and sisters and their struggles, without devolving into legalistic practices? How can the questions, *"Am I loving God? Am I loving people?"* be used corporately to make decisions that honor freedom in Christ as well as help less mature believers? What is the danger of church leaders being too specific about what all believers should do in every situation?

_____

_____

_____

_____

_____

_____

_____

_____

_____

_____

_____

Journal: Did you grow up in a home or church with strict standards, or in an environment where everything was permissible? Has your Christian life tended more toward legalism or license? What damage have these extremes caused in your life or in the lives of believers you know? What are some potential pitfalls for you, personally, that lead you to choose higher standards in order to avoid them? How can you consistently walk in a scriptural balance that honors Christ and His Word?

_____

_____

_____

_____

_____

_____

_____

_____

_____

_____

_____

Action: Pick an issue such as dancing, drinking, tattoos, modest clothing, etc., and separately interview two mature believers who have differing views on this issue.

Possible questions:

1. What was your experience with this issue growing up or prior to salvation?

2. How has God led you in this area?

3. What personal guidelines do you have regarding this issue?

4. How would you counsel a new believer who was uncertain how to honor God in this area of their life?

5. What would you say to a fellow Christian who disagrees with your stand on this issue?

Use their answers as a springboard for your own prayer and study regarding this issue.

Chapter Five Notes

CHAPTER SIX

Joyful Community

Therefore if you have any encouragement from being united with Christ, if any comfort from his love, if any common sharing in the Spirit, if any tenderness and compassion, then make my joy complete by being like-minded, having the same love, being one in spirit and of one mind. Do nothing out of selfish ambition or vain conceit. Rather, in humility value others above yourselves, not looking to your own interests but each of you to the interests of the others.

—Philippians 2:1–4

A healthy church is made up of individuals who actively love one another and desire to live and worship together in community.

Anytime you get a group of people together in the same place, over a long period of time, conflict is bound to rear its ugly head. You might start out doing pretty well, but before long, sin enters the room and causes all kinds of problems. John is annoyed by Henry, so John gets snarky. Judy and Dan break up, and Dan asks out Karen, but Judy and Karen have to keep getting along together. Someone is left out or says something out of anger, or someone gets jealous. Before long, there are a myriad of awkward feelings and touchy situations.

The trouble with a lot of churches is they often *feel* good on the surface. Fellowship time is full of smiles and handshakes and asking, "How are you this week?" For one hour a week, everyone looks clean and shiny, and they all get along. But once we get in our cars to go home, our real feelings come out. And we are jealous, petty, resentful, bitter sinners deep down inside.

When nonbelievers look at church people, they often see a lot of fake relationships. They see the shiny façade while knowing that underneath things are still broken. And we Christians don't do much to fight against that image. It's hard to open up about our sin. It's hard to forgive past hurts, real or imagined. It's hard to love the other broken people around us because we are broken ourselves.

But as we study what the Bible says community is to look like, we see a really beautiful picture. Imagine being a part of a group of people who love Jesus so passionately, they are quick to forgive and they work to be more patient and considerate. They look for ways to care for each other. If someone doesn't have enough, they are quick to contribute. They are open and honest about their sin and together strive to be more Christlike. I don't know about you, but my heart yearns for every church to be that kind of community!

We Are One Because God Is One

Yeah, but that community can't really exist, can it? Actually, the Bible tells us it can. The early church was often touted as being a shining example of this kind of holiness. I know that was thousands of years ago, but God still calls us and can empower us to be unified communities.

When Jesus was in the Garden of Gethsemane, He was doing some pretty intense praying. He prayed for Himself, and then He prayed for His disciples, and finally he prayed for all believers—and it is really important that we understand what He prayed for us to be. John 17:22 says that Jesus prayed, "I have given them the glory that you gave me, *that they may be one* as we are one" (emphasis added).

Did you key in on how we are to be unified? We are called to be one, like the Trinity is one. In fact, God is a community: He is three in one, and He has been that way since the very beginning.

In Deuteronomy 6:4, God is speaking to His people before handing down the Ten Commandments, and He says this: "Hear O Israel: the LORD our God, the LORD is *one*." The word *one* in this verse is the Hebrew word *'echad.*[4] Interestingly, that is the same word used when God spoke of Adam and Eve being joined together:[5] "…a man shall leave his father and mother and be joined to his wife, and the two shall become *one* flesh" (Genesis 2:24, emphasis added). How cool is it, that marriage is a symbolic representation of who God is—a community of one!

Trying to understand and grasp the concept of the Trinity is a difficult theological task. And, let me just say, until we find ourselves in His presence one day, we may never understand it fully. However, I have heard many illustrations and anecdotes over the years that try to help people come to a better understanding, including pretzels (three holes, one snack) and eggs (shell, whites, and yolk).

However, even though it's still imperfect, the best analogy I've heard comes from nature—God's creation itself, the most abundant resource on the planet: water. H_2O is the chemical symbol for water. H_2O, when it's at room temperature, is water in liquid form. That water can hydrate, wash, refresh, and so much more. When you freeze H_2O, you get ice. Ice is a different form, a solid, and is useful for different tasks. It can heal, cool, keep things fresh longer, etc. Now, if you add heat to H_2O, it takes on another form, steam. Steam can now be used to disinfect, cook, de-wrinkle, sanitize, and more.

Water, ice, and steam are all H_2O. Though the chemical makeup never changes, certain other properties do. This is a lot like God, Jesus, and the Holy Spirit: each one of them is God, but they take different forms in order to complete different tasks for the Kingdom. Somewhat similarly, our calling is to be individuals when it comes to our own personal gifts and talents, yet to be unified in fulfilling our Kingdom purpose as the church.

Yummy Is Messy

One thing we need to understand from the beginning is that doing life together as a community is going to be messy. I like to say that this kind of community is a "yummy" community. There are lots of flavors and textures. There are things that work well together and things that maybe sometimes don't generally go together. These things can be combined to create something wonderful and delicious. At NBC On Main we like to call it "yummy church."

But yummy is messy. We have already established my love for cooking. When I get in the kitchen, I really go to town. As I pursue creating a delicious meal, I generally make a big ole mess (just ask my wife!). When I mix together ingredients for a loaf of bread, I spill a bit of flour over the edge of the measuring cup. Sauce gets splattered while I stir. The dish in the oven bubbles over.

Church is the same. We are messy! We are broken. We do stupid things. This is when church gets hard. But, the Bible doesn't say that when we get to know the other people in our church and our toes get stepped on that we should go find a new church.

Colossians 3:12–13 says, "Therefore, as God's chosen people, holy and dearly loved, clothe yourselves with compassion, kindness, humility, gentleness and patience. Bear with each other and forgive one another if any of you has a grievance against someone. Forgive as the Lord forgave you."

Did you catch that? I love the image of us clothing ourselves with these things. It's a conscious choice to wake up, take a shower, get dressed for church, and then pull on your socks of compassion, your kindness hat, your humble pants, your gentleness gloves, and your patience glasses. Then we get in the car and go to church, ready to love and serve others rather than be seen as some dignified individual who attends the "right" church.

Unity Means All of Us Are All In

If someone came to me and said he wanted to write a check for a million dollars to my church with the stipulation that he never had to serve anywhere ever again, I'd refuse the money. I really would. There is so much blessing in serving that I could never enable someone to miss out on it. Not to mention, giving in and of itself should never come with stipulations; if it does, it becomes a purchase, not a gift.

Healthy believers don't just go to church to be served. They understand that they aren't going to a theater where they will be entertained and someone else will sweep up their spilled popcorn after they leave. Healthy believers recognize that they are a part of a family and, out of their love for their family members, are eager to lend a hand.

I want to take this a step further. So often, people want to go to church on Sunday morning and then live the rest of the week however they want. It's like they're paying their dues so that they can be left to their own devices. When something happens at church they don't like, they grumble about it. When someone upsets them, they tell whoever will listen about the other person's shortcomings.

Being a part of a healthy church means being all in. It means that you don't just listen to the worship music and sing along, feeling uncomfortable until you can sit down. Rather, you understand that the people around you need to see others worshiping the Lord, so you close your eyes and do your best to love others by making joyful worship normal. It means that you join a small group, if that's what your pastor says needs to happen, because you want to support the church's initiatives even if it's not "your thing." It means getting to church early and talking to the new person who sits near you, even asking her to coffee later so she can feel welcome, rather than show up late, slink in, and sit near the back with your friends.

It means asking yourself, *"How can I love, serve, and give as a part of my church community?"* It's putting aside your own agenda and humbly trusting in the leadership of your home church. It's inviting the people in your life to come experience your church family in the hope that they will want to be a part of this tremendous community and, eventually, God's family.

Forgive Now

You drive up to the family reunion and scan the cars parked in the lot. When you see Uncle Joe's car, you roll your eyes. *"Oh, goodie. He's here again this year."* Maybe you can avoid getting sucked into another political tirade.

Families seem to be full of people we love but don't always like very much. And, if we were all honest, it can be exactly the same arriving at church on a Sunday morning. There are people who are fine from a distance, but when you get close, old tensions flare up. Sometimes it even starts in the parking lot! "So-and-so parked in the visitor space again. Isn't she selfish?"

First John 4:20 says, "Whoever claims to love God yet

hates a brother or sister is a liar. For whoever does not love their brother and sister, whom they have seen, cannot love God, whom they have not seen." Ouch! That really puts things in perspective, doesn't it?

Let me be frank with you: if you are a part of a church for any period of time, you are going to end up hurting others and being hurt by someone else. It is the nature of relationships involving sinful people. It's a guarantee. Keeping those hurts from turning into bitterness and resentment, and even anger, is a difficult thing to do.

It's easy to say, "Oh, I forgive that person," while not being willing to really put the hurt aside. You can smile and nod at each other, but you just aren't quite going to be unified or connected again like you once were.

And yet, that restored connection is exactly what God wants. In Matthew 5:23–24, Jesus commands us, "Therefore, if you are offering your gift at the altar and there remember that your brother or sister has something against you, leave your gift there in front of the altar. First go and be reconciled to them; then come and offer your gift." Did you catch that this is about what *you* have done wrong? It isn't about what the *other* person has done wrong, but about your own sin.

If you're in church, burning holes in the back of the head of someone sitting in front of you, you are the one who is sinning. Even if that person wronged you, you have something that must be dealt with and you need to confess. That's the funny thing about unforgiveness: when we fail to forgive, we sin. It is a serious equalizer. You sinned when you wronged me, but I've sinned by not forgiving.

As if we need it, another very important reason why we

need to be forgiving is that cracks in our community affect our outreach. If we don't live together in unity, we cannot spread the gospel efficiently. New believers who enter the church might think it's okay to talk about each other behind their backs, take sides over what color the new carpet should be, or refuse to be a part of a committee because *that person* is on it. We cannot be an example of the unity of God, Jesus, and the Spirit if we all simply want what we want, and want it now, at all costs. This is hypocrisy, and it will kill the body of Christ.

Remember Jesus' prayer I shared earlier in the chapter? Jesus prayed "that they may be *one* as we are one" (John 17:11, emphasis added). We have already established that He was talking about us—about believers, about church. But He also told us why! The next bit of the passage is crucial: He said, "Then the world will know that you sent me" (John 17:23). That's it.

The key to reaching the world with the gospel isn't a tract, a song, a t-shirt, an evangelist, or a megachurch. The key to real evangelism and reaching the masses comes down to the unity of the church. It really is that simple. We can't reach the world if we can't get along.

The great theologian A. W. Tozer said it like this: "Has it ever occurred to you that one hundred pianos all tuned to the same fork are automatically tuned to each other? They are of one accord by being tuned, not to each other, but to another standard to which each one must individually bow."[6] We must keep our eyes focused on Jesus *together*. If we are all "in tune" with Him, we will be "in tune" with one another.

Chapter Six Questions

Am I? Are you naturally a loner, or do you value community? What aspects of community do you find to be the most challenging? When the unity of your community is broken, do you strive to repair those relationships, or do you run from the conflict?

_____

_____

_____

_____

_____

_____

_____

_____

_____

Are We? In what ways does your church excel at building community? Where are there divisions, tensions, and general messiness? What are some ways you can encourage people to keep working toward community even in the difficult times? What are some ways you can bridge natural gaps such as age, marital status, and background to help your community appreciate each other and the unique gifts and story that God has given to each of you?

_____

_____

_____

_____

_____

_____

_____

_____

_____

_____

_____

Journal: Describe a time when you experienced true Christian community, or what is often described as "doing life together." What are some of the qualities that it takes to be a part of that type of community?

_____

_____

_____

_____

_____

_____

_____

_____

_____

_____

_____

_____

Action: Whom do you need to forgive? What is keeping you from reaching out to that person and making things right? Whom do you need to ask for forgiveness, and how can you try to reconcile with that person? Read Ephesians 4:32 and Colossians 3:13, and purpose to repair your community as soon as possible.

Chapter Six Notes

_____

_____

_____

_____

_____

_____

_____

_____

_____

_____

_____

_____

_____

_____

_____

_____

_____

_____

_____

_____

_____

_____

_____

CHAPTER SEVEN

Engaging Sin

For we know that our old self was crucified with [Jesus] so that the body ruled by sin might be done away with, that we should no longer be slaves to sin—because anyone who has died has been set free from sin.
—Romans 6:6–7

A healthy church is made up of individuals who are willing to engage one another and be engaged over sin.

Maggie was four years old and rather a handful. She was one of those kids who is quick on the uptake and full of mischief. At the end of the day, her grandma would gladly put Maggie in her mom's car and go back in the house for a rest.

One day, Maggie was downstairs playing with some old toys. Now, these toys had originally come from the Dollar Store and had been played with by older cousins plenty of times. But Maggie was too little to understand that.

Grandma was fixing lunch in the kitchen when in came a sobbing Maggie from the playroom, holding a plastic doll that had broken in half.

"Grandma! I so sorry!" she bawled.

Grandma sat down, took Maggie in her lap, and assured her that it was all right. This was not a valuable toy, and it was bound to break eventually. Before long, Maggie's tears were dried and she was skipping off to play again.

A short time later, though, Maggie got herself into some real trouble. Grandma put her in time-out, and the sounds of Maggie's angry cries reverberated through the house. But by the time Grandma went to get her, Maggie had learned a lesson about what to do and what not to do. And once again, Grandma gladly sent Maggie home with her mother and went to bed early.

Assess Honestly

First John 1:9 is familiar to a lot of us: "If we confess our sins, [God] is faithful and just and will forgive us our sins and purify us from all unrighteousness." But we aren't quite as familiar with verse 10: "If we claim we have not sinned, we make [God] out to be a liar and his word is not in us."

Healthy followers of Christ are able to look at themselves and honestly assess where they are in all areas of their walk with God, and they do so regularly. They don't just look at their strengths and ignore their weaknesses. "I'm tithing, serving on the greeting team, and praying twice a day. I'm fine." Nope. That's just not how it works.

Think of this in terms of physical health. If I go to the gym and only ever run on the treadmill, I'm not building muscle. If I only lift weights with my arms, my legs aren't going to get stronger. If I only eat right but never exercise, I'm not really pursuing good health.

We must be willing to assess ourselves honestly, without giving excuses. It's one thing to examine the triggers for your sin. In fact, it's vital that you do. But to refuse to work on something because of the trigger is wrong. A man might look at pornography when he's stressed. Recognizing that stress brings on that temptation is beneficial. Saying that it's fine to look at porn because of stress is pretending that the sin is okay—and therein lies the problem.

I have struggled personally with pride. Over the years, I've experienced some successes as a communicator. And at times, I've allowed those successes to swell into prideful thinking that pushes aside humility. It's often tempting to chase those things that build up my pride. This is made even more difficult by the fact that my love language is words of encouragement. I benefit greatly when people tell me what I'm doing right; it spurs me on to greater things. But it also has the potential to feed my pride. Being encouraged is a good thing; becoming prideful is sinful. Balancing the two—or better yet, allowing the Spirit to balance it for you—is healthy.

Confession Is Critical

There is such power in confessing our sin. I'm not sure why it works the way it does. Sin that is kept hidden is able to grow and fester, a lot like mold in a dark, damp room. Even if we merely confess our sin to God, without including some honest accountability by our confession to others, that sin can maintain some power over us. Yet, when we go to a brother or sister and confess our sin out loud, it begins to lose its power over us. Then, together, we can begin the journey of overcoming.

We must be able to stand in front of someone and say, "I screwed up." Our churches need to be places where it is normal and healthy to confess our sin to each other. We must be willing to open up our hearts and air out the secret places without the fear of judgment or condemnation. James 5:16 says, "Therefore confess your sins to each other and pray for each other so that you may be healed. The prayer of a righteous person is powerful and effective."

When people who are new to this kind of confession first imagine themselves telling their sins to other people, they tend to recoil. *"You want me to do what?"* We all have sins that we never dreamed of talking about to anyone else. We can't even imagine how people will see us if they know the truth.

But we are all sinners. Did you catch that? We are *all* sinners. We have all done things we are ashamed of—sometimes through our actions or our words, and sometimes by our lack of words or actions. When we live in a community of people who are willing to confess sins and be confronted about sins we don't see in ourselves, we are humbly acknowledging we are all in this pursuit together. We are sinners in need of a Savior. And, let me tell you, that is something unbelievers find irresistible.

Christians are often labeled as hypocrites because we declare that perfection is required while being unable to ever achieve that perfection ourselves. When we confess our sins earnestly, and create an atmosphere not of sinning, but of confession, we are no longer hypocrites, because we are admitting our need for Christ's work on the cross.

Earnest Repentance

The thing I love most about that story about little Maggie from the beginning of the chapter is her earnest repentance. Not only did this little girl run straight to her grandmother when she broke a toy, but she was also honestly sorry. She didn't hide the toy and hope not to get in trouble. She was afraid Grandma would be upset but still went to her, wanting to have her mistake made right.

As Christians who confess regularly, we get really permissive at times, don't we? Someone in small group confesses anger, and we all nod and say, "Thanks for sharing. How brave of you to open up." But we don't always get around to repentance. Sometimes, it is just easier to speak and not truly deal with the sin. Other times, we don't necessarily want to require repentance of others because we aren't mature enough to desire repentance ourselves. But that is an unhealthy view. Remember, it is the kindness of the Lord that leads us to repentance (Romans 2:4).

Confession is owning up to our sin. Repentance is turning away from it. We aren't ever going to find complete freedom from our sin without both of these things. I get so annoyed when I go somewhere to deal with an issue and the person simply, flippantly says, "Sorry." It's easy to say the words and shrug the shoulders. It's even easy at times to look at our sin and realize we've messed up, as long as we aren't required to actually do something differently.

Think about this: How angry would you be if your son or daughter borrowed the car and got a dent in the side, came to you and apologized, and then went out and did the same thing again the next day? One time might be excusable, but repeated dents just means carelessness. There is no effort to change the behavior or to do better, so the actions of the child expose that his or her confessions don't mean much.

If we stop at confession, we fail extravagantly. Confession is not enough. We must turn away from our sin. Whether or not we want to, we must get up and walk away from it. We walk out of the bedroom, we walk out of the bar, we leave the conversation, we get away from the job. We ask God to give us the strength and courage to flee from temptation. First Corinthians 10:13 says, "No temptation has overtaken you except what is common to mankind. And God is faithful; he will not let you be tempted beyond what you can bear. But when you are tempted, he will also provide a way out so that you can endure it."

Engaging Others

Imagine you are a doctor. A woman comes in complaining of not feeling well, so you run tests, which reveal she has cancer. You can't in good conscience put on a smile and say, "No, you're fine," the next time she comes in. You have an obligation to tell her what's wrong so that she can pursue healing.

Similarly, this woman isn't likely to refuse treatment because it's going to be painful. It is doubtful she is going to respond with, "You're going to open me up and remove the tumor? I'm going to have a scar and it's going to hurt a lot while the wound heals? No, thanks. I'll take my chances with the cancer." Of course not! The cancer must be addressed before it causes her more pain and suffering, or even takes her life.

Yet we are so reluctant, as Christians, to engage others over their sin. I will be the first to admit that even as a pastor, this is something that's really difficult for me. I get concerned, and even anxious, that people are going to be upset with me, tell others how awful I am, and possibly leave the church. But, I cannot lead or love well if I make my decisions based on how they might respond.

I know that a lot of people have fears about confession and engagement on both the delivering and receiving end. The Bible is clear about how we are to approach one another. But when Jesus was teaching on how to confront your neighbor over sin in Matthew 17, He was proceeding with a certain understanding: He was speaking to people who were living together in community. They were doing life together. They accepted that each person was there to bring joy and life and love to the next.

We must grab hold of this kind of community, and it's the way our churches need to be. When we connect with a church, we should do so with an understanding that we are all there to make one another's lives better. We all need Jesus. We all need help. Keeping this loving, focused, and humble attitude will help aid in the process.

It is likely we have all dealt with rejection when it comes to confrontation. There is potential for this to happen as long as sin is in the world and in our lives. When we are living in sin, we rarely want it pointed out by others. We certainly don't need "that sinner" calling us out. But please remember this: in a healthy church, we are *all* sinners. Life is messy, and we need each other. If we discount every person who sins as unable to speak into our lives, what happens? Right—no one can speak into our lives. That is just unhealthy. So, however unpleasant, engaging and being engaged are a major component for both individuals and the entire body of Christ being healthier.

The fact is, we are not loving our brothers and sisters well if we don't help them to see their sin clearly. When we see sin in the lives of others in our church, we have an obligation to confront them lovingly. If we let sin slide, we are allowing something hurtful to grow in the lives of the people around us.

Don't think for a minute that keeping the peace is what real peace is about. In Matthew 5:9, Jesus says, "Blessed are the peacemakers." Make a note, He did not say "peace-*keepers*." I believe, out of perceived kindness, avoidance, or genuine fear of conflict, we often avoid having the hard conversations. We sometimes justify it in the name of keeping the peace. Avoiding sensitive topics isn't helping the people in our lives to have deep inner peace, knowing that they are right with God. If you don't confront someone, you are partially responsible for their unhealthy lifestyle. We must be willing to risk the chance we might offend someone in order to lovingly fight for their freedom and their joy, and ultimately see real love in our church families .

WORKBOOK

Chapter Seven Questions

Am I? How often do you examine your life and confess your sin? Do you own up and repent, or do you look for excuses to justify your sin? When and why could you be helped by acknowledging to another believer your struggle with a particular sin and asking for their prayer and accountability? When and where is such sharing inappropriate?

_____

_____

_____

_____

_____

_____

_____

_____

_____

_____

_____

Are We? Is your church a safe place for people to share their struggles, or do they feel that they will be judged, condemned, or marginalized if they are honest about their sins and problems? How can your church create an environment that encourages authenticity and gives appropriate settings for people to share?

_____

_____

_____

_____

_____

_____

_____

_____

_____

_____

_____

Journal: Has anyone ever confronted you over sin in your life? Did they do so in a biblical manner or in a self-righteous one? Have you ever confronted another believer over sin? Was your attitude Christlike, and your approach biblical? What can you learn from these experiences to help you engage correctly with others over sin?

_____

_____

_____

_____

_____

_____

_____

_____

_____

_____

_____

Action: Read the account in 2 Samuel 12 of Nathan confronting David over his sin, as well as David's response in Psalm 51. What can you learn about loving rebuke and sincere repentance from these passages?

Chapter Seven Notes

_____

_____

_____

_____

_____

_____

_____

_____

_____

_____

_____

_____

_____

_____

_____

_____

_____

_____

_____

_____

_____

_____

_____

_____

CHAPTER EIGHT

Discipline Discerningly

If your brother or sister sins, go and point out their fault, just between the two of you. If they listen to you, you have won them over. But if they will not listen, take one or two others along, so that 'every matter may be established by the testimony of two or three witnesses.' If they still refuse to listen, tell it to the church; and if they refuse to listen even to the church, treat them as you would a pagan or a tax collector.

—Matthew 18:15–17

A healthy church is made up of individuals who engage in discerning church discipline.

When you go to a hospital, you expect to see people who are sick or injured, right? It wouldn't make sense to see the waiting room full of people who are in perfect health. That's not what a hospital is for.

Similarly, church doesn't exist for sinless people. They'd be pretty empty if that were true. Yet, for some reason, Christians like to pretend that they aren't sinful.

We like to give the impression that our churches are full of folks who have it all together. That's not what a church is for.

We are all sinners. In fact, if you read through the Gospels, you'll find that the people who sought out Jesus were almost always outcasts in desperate need. Without sin and suffering, we wouldn't need Jesus.

A healthy Christian is someone who is actively working on his or her sin issues. We've talked about the importance of confession and repenting. Healthy believers regularly examine their hearts, their motives, and their actions and continually strive to be more Christlike.

However, there are some situations in which this isn't happening. People who claim to be followers of Christ, who are knowingly engaging in ongoing sin, need to be lovingly confronted. Unfortunately, as we discussed in Chapter Seven, healthy church discipline does not happen very often, if at all.

The Goal of Church Discipline

The ultimate goal of church discipline is to end up with better, healthier people. It *must* be about restoration. The church should begin with a desire for all believers to be the awesome people God created them to be. It isn't to chase away sinners. We don't want to leave a trail of broken ex-church members scattered behind us. We want people to see their sin, be grieved by it, and turn away from that sin to find healing and freedom. We want people to be restored. The church as a whole has lost its way when it comes to this particular practice. We have carved out canyons of scattered former leaders, pastors, and ministers, cast out and left behind due to one sin or another. This is not God's plan.

The church is to be made up of followers or disciples of Jesus. Read through the Gospels. You'll see Him repeatedly confronting people about their wrong heart issues. What you won't see is Jesus only spending time with the ultra-religious people (Matthew 9:10–11). In fact, the Pharisees, who were the Jewish religious elite, were most often earning a reprimand from Jesus (Matthew 23:12–14).

Everything that God makes has integrity. If you cut open a watermelon, you find watermelon inside, not grapes or an orange. You have never peeled a banana and expected to find a walnut inside. As Gods chosen people, we must learn to be honest and truthful about what is really going on inside. When people come into our churches, they should see sinners who are living their lives trying to be more like Christ. We should be a reflection of who God is. And God doesn't shy away from dealing with ongoing sin issues even if they will hurt for a little while.

What Discipline Is Not

Before you decide that you'll never be a part of church discipline, let me clarify what discipline is not.

Discerning discipline is not an excuse to point out every single sin you see someone commit. This isn't a place to keep a list of sins and then run around tattling on people. We aren't to go and confront the pastor whenever our toes get stepped on in a sermon. In fact, hurt feelings are not necessarily a reason to discipline someone.

Discerning discipline is not an excuse to gossip. I recently heard the definition of *gossip* as "telling someone about someone else's sins." It's not loving to tell other people about someone's sins. "Well, Judy can't be blamed for missing church since she's an alcoholic." "I can't go to Dennis's birthday celebration because I don't want people to think I approve of his gambling addiction." That is absolutely not what discipline is about.

Discerning discipline is not about kicking people out of the church. The goal is to draw people to Jesus, not to push them away. Yes, the Bible does say that under certain circumstances, someone might be asked to leave the church, but that happens only in limited situations and if the people around that person have done things the right way according to Scripture.

Discerning discipline does not give the church permission to air out people's sins for all to see. I once heard about a church where two of the teens were having sex and the girl found out that she was pregnant. The pastor had the two stand up in front of the church on a Sunday morning and confess their sin in front of everyone. Can you imagine how mortifying that must have been for them? That isn't the goal! If those two had already confessed their sin to the appropriate people in their lives and were repentant, their sin didn't need to be discussed for all to hear. Quite frankly, that poor girl was going to have her sin made obvious in a few months' time. She didn't need to be publicly shamed.

Discerning discipline is not focused on one kind of sin

over another. Sure, some sins are more public and have a bigger immediate effect on our lives. Sexual sin is often this way, though I'm sorry to say that I've seen a lot of churches eagerly discipline homosexual sin and completely ignore heterosexual sin. All sin damages our lives and can affect the lives of those in our community. All sin keeps us from a healthy relationship with Christ.

What Discerning Discipline Is

Let me give you an example of how one church correctly handled a sin issue with discerning discipline.

John played drums in the worship band. He had been a member of the church for years. When John and his girlfriend got engaged, they moved in together. Adam, one of the church's pastors and a friend of John's, went to coffee with John. He asked John if he was having sex with his fiancé. John admitted that they were. Adam humbly, lovingly pointed out that this was not in accordance with God's teachings. He proposed a few solutions for helping John and his girlfriend to move out until they got married.

Unfortunately, John grew angry. He didn't like being told what to do and had no intentions of giving up sex with his fiancé. So Adam privately went to Allan, another pastor in the church, and the two of them approached John about this sin issue. Again, John refused to acknowledge the sin in his life and make efforts toward repentance.

After several attempts to work with John, it became apparent that he wasn't going to change. Therefore, Adam and Allan spoke to the congregation. They explained that John, whom they loved dearly, was choosing to engage in sinful behavior without repentance. John was asked to step down from the worship team, and from other positions of leadership in the church. At this point, John's resentment got the best of him and he walked away from the church.

However, Adam and Allan asked the church to continue loving and praying for John. The church was asked to continue to reach out to John, to treat him like anyone else when they ran into him, and always to let him know he was welcome at church anytime.

Over the next few months, Adam kept in contact with John. He came to Adam's Super Bowl party. The two men went for coffee and caught up on each other's lives. As time went by, John realized how much he missed the church. He hadn't seen his friends who'd been like family to him since he'd stopped coming. And even more, he began to realize how empty his spiritual life was.

Eventually, John came back to Adam and Allan and opened up about his relationship with his fiancé. He confessed and repented, and moved into Allan's spare bedroom until his wedding day. Eventually, not only did John reconnect with his church family, but he also began playing the drums for the worship team again. That is an example of how discerning church discipline plays out to restoration!

Do you see what happened here? Let me point out the things that occurred that were in line with the Bible:

Adam first went alone and confronted John about his sin. He did it in a humble, loving way with the hope that John would repent and grow closer to Christ. And when John refused, Adam didn't throw up his hands and give up. He didn't tell everyone who would listen about what had happened. He kept loving and praying for John.

Adam then quietly went to another solid brother, and the two of them together confronted John. This is a really important step. Coming with another spiritually mature believer means that you have someone who can listen and let you know if you're out of line or taking things too far. It means that there's a witness when you need to go to the church leaders about this person. And it also tells the person you're confronting that someone else knows what's going on. As I said before, sin has power when it's dark and hidden. Bringing along a second witness helps draw it out into the light, where it can be diffused.

When Adam and Allan went to the church, they weren't trying to shame John. They didn't ask the church to shun him. Instead, they were loving him and still hoping to draw him back to Christ.

After John left the church, he was treated with kindness. Adam continued to try and reach out to him for restoration. The process took time. It took forgiveness. It took mature believers consistently being the hands and feet of Jesus to John.

In the end, John was able to see that he was missing something. Discipline isn't discipline if there are no consequences. Telling John that he was wrong to have sex with his fiancé wasn't going to bring repentance. John had to go through the entire process of discipline before he was in a situation in which he was able to realize the cost of his sin.

Three Reasons Why Churches Don't Discipline

The first reason why churches don't discipline correctly is that we often have the wrong motives. Whether we're acting out of superiority, a desire to control, or just about anything other than humble love, it's easy to have the wrong motives when we deal with discipline.

Remember, we are only called to go through this process if the person in question has sin that he or she isn't actively confessing and putting forth effort to repent. There are going to be times when each of us makes a mistake. It might take a lot of do-overs before we start making good progress. However, there's a difference between an alcoholic having one drink, when under a great deal of stress and temptation, and an alcoholic hanging out at the bar every single night. We are to take reasonable actions to move toward freedom from sin. If that isn't happening, then it's time to look into the process of loving and discerning discipline.

The second reason is weak leadership. There are times when it is really hard for the leaders of a church to pursue discerning discipline. Maybe the member in question contributes financially in a big way or is very popular or plays a big role in the church. Sometimes the leaders fear losing their congregations over the issue. Plenty of churches have fallen apart this way.

However, if we love our brothers and sisters, we don't want them to suffer the consequences of sin. Ignoring sin is problematic. It is detrimental to our loved ones. If we are helping each other to see our sin on a regular basis, the hope is that we will appreciate this and normalize it. Then the process of church discipline doesn't have to go all the way to the extreme. Instead, we will examine our hearts and appreciate the person who confronted us, because we can grow closer to God.

The final reason we don't often exercise discerning discipline is a poor understanding of Scripture. Either we aren't spending time with God so that the Holy Spirit can show us things that need to be addressed, or we don't really understand how serious sin is. We assume it's someone else's responsibility to deal with the issue.

Real, discerning discipline occurs with truth, love, grace, and repentance, and finishes with restoration. It is always done with the goal of drawing people to Christ. It is not about lifting one person up, above another, or pushing someone else down. And the hope is always that approaching someone lovingly about his or her sin will result in quick repentance and restoration without the full process.

We are all called to keep each other accountable. In churches where this is part of everyday life, it is invaluable. We are called to help pick up the weight of each other's sin and to help our brothers and sisters stand up under temptation.

WORKBOOK

Chapter Eight Questions

Am I? *A healthy Christian is someone who is actively working on his or her sin issues.* How are you doing this in your life? If you are not, why not? To whom are you accountable, and are you transparent with this person(s)? Do you welcome other believers speaking hard truths into your life?

_____

_____

_____

_____

_____

_____

_____

_____

_____

Are We? Does your church practice church discipline? If not, which of the three reasons given might be the hindrance? If so, is it being done in a humble, loving way, or in a way that will unnecessarily shame and distance the offenders?

_____

_____

_____

_____

_____

_____

_____

_____

_____

_____

_____

Journal: Why is confronting sin an expression of genuine love? How is this countercultural in our tolerance-obsessed society? What are some of the consequences of churches failing to deal with sin in their midst?

_____

_____

_____

_____

_____

_____

_____

_____

_____

_____

_____

_____

Action: Read Matthew 18:15–20 and ask the leaders of your church how and when they apply this for the formal process of church discipline. If you are one of the church leaders, plan a time to talk with the congregation about your church's process of church discipline, and when and why it might be used. Read these accounts of how sin was addressed in the early church. What can you learn from each?

- Peter confronting Ananias and Sapphira (Acts 5:1–11)

- Paul confronting Peter (Galatians 2:11–14)

- Paul confronting sexual sin in the Corinthian church (1 Corinthians 5; 2 Corinthians 2:5–11)

Chapter Eight Notes

_____

_____

_____

_____

_____

_____

_____

_____

_____

_____

_____

_____

_____

_____

_____

_____

_____

_____

_____

_____

_____

_____

_____

_____

_____

CHAPTER NINE

Open-Handed

Remember this: Whoever sows sparingly will also reap sparingly, and whoever sows generously will also reap generously. Each of you should give what you have decided in your heart to give, not reluctantly or under compulsion, for God loves a cheerful giver. And God is able to bless you abundantly, so that in all things at all times, having all that you need, you will abound in every good work.
—2 Corinthians 9:6–8

A healthy church is made up of individuals who are open-handed.

I want you to picture two workers. We'll call the first John and the second Jane. Both John and Jane work at the exact same job. They make the same amount of money and have the same boss. Each of these employees turns in the same amount of work every week.

However, there's a big difference between them. John is in his seat at eight o'clock sharp every morning. He leaves at five o'clock on the button and takes his allotted one-hour lunch break without fail. He does exactly what is asked of him and nothing more.

Well, in fact, John does do something more: he complains. If his boss asks him to help train a co-worker, John is upset about it and lets everyone know. When he was "volun-told" to do some extra paperwork, he was not happy and made everyone around him miserable.

Jane, on the other hand, looks at her work rather differently. She often ends up at the office a bit late because she's talking with a fellow employee who's going through a hard time. When Carol was eight months pregnant, Jane made sure to carry Carol's heavy box of reports for her without being asked. When asked to do a little extra paperwork, Jane agreed readily and even gave up some of her lunch hour in order to make sure it was done on time.

Now, if you were the boss of these two workers, who would you want to fill the position of manager when it came open? Both Jane and John do their work well. However, Jane comes to work with an open-handed approach. She recognizes that this is her job and it's within her boss's rights to ask her to take on more tasks. She views her fellow workers as a part of her job, too. John does what's asked of him grudgingly. His boss is completely right to ask him to take on more tasks, but John grouses about it. In the end, it comes down to attitude.

In 2 Corinthians 9:6–8, Paul explained how our attitude should be when it comes to giving. He told us to be cheerful and generous, not reluctant and merely dutiful. In fact, the word *cheerful* in this passage is *hilaros*[7]—the Greek origin for the English word *hilarious*.[8] Is your giving so generous that you and even others around you might find it hysterical or hilarious? Our natural response to God's generosity to us should be exuberant generosity to others.

A lot of times, when we're talking about generosity, pastors focus only on financial generosity. In this chapter, though, I want you to think about other resources, too. Think about your time, your energy, your compassion, and—yes—also your money.

Owners Versus Stewards

First Peter 4:10 tells us, "Each of you should use whatever gift you have received to serve others, as faithful stewards of God's grace in its various forms." In Luke chapter 16 (NKJV), Jesus tells the parable of a faithful steward who is rewarded by his master.

The term *steward* isn't one we use very often anymore, is it? When we see it in the Bible, it refers to someone who works for a master. The steward handles all of the master's business but doesn't own any of it. Think of a manager at a restaurant. The manager runs the place, divvies out the responsibilities, and is charged with making sure the establishment is profitable. But it does not belong to the manager; the owner receives the profits. Conversely, if the restaurant loses money or is not profitable, the owner is likely to take action, and fire the manager.

This is how God tells us to think about the things in our lives. Even if we believe it is *our* money, *our* homes, *our* loved ones, *our* time, *our* health, we are not the owners— we are the stewards. Have you ever stopped to think that we essentially rent everything we spend our money on? We'll use it for a while, and eventually it will go on to someone else.

It's imperative that we shift our thinking about all of our possessions and resources, material and otherwise. God owns it all and is blessing us with it, trusting us to use it for His glory. It isn't ours at all, and if God decides that it's in our best interest to no longer have something, He can take it back at any time.

Let's take a look at a parable in the Bible that outlines this principle with clarity. Take note, however: this parable is not all candy and roses. In Matthew 25, there is a story about a master who entrusted three of his servants with varying degrees of finances. To one he gave five bags of gold, to the next he gave two, and to the final servant he gave one.

The master went away and then returned at a much later time, at which point he invited all three servants to come and return his wealth to him. The servant with five bags returned ten to the master. The servant with two returned four to the master. Each had worked to double the fortune of his master. The final servant gave back only the single bag of gold—without increase—that he had originally received.

The response of the master to this last servant was completely different from his response to the first two servants. To *both* of the servants who worked to double his gifts, he responded by applauding their efforts and inviting them to join in *all* of his wealth. But the final servant was given a stern reprimand and was ordered to be tossed out to an awful place.

Now, we need to be diligent in our understanding of a few things. This is a story about us! The master is God.

Every resource we are entrusted with is His. When He returns, we will give an account of all we have done with His gifts to us. When we are good stewards, what follows is blessings beyond what we could imagine. Notice that the final servant didn't steal anything; he didn't lose what was given to him. He simply brought back what the master had given him—but the master's response was critical.

We must understand the heart of our Master and know Him well. When we choose to work hard, obey, and follow Him, the blessings will come and the Kingdom work will flourish. If we hide our blessings, or sit on them, we will be cast out. I know it seems harsh, but we must understand that our lives, our finances, our homes, and even our children are all gifts and blessings from God. He can take what is His at any time, which in no way contradicts the fact that He is loving, just, and merciful.

God is a good Father (Matthew 7:11). When we choose to live our lives with our hands and hearts wide open, it is a display of our trust in Him. It is acknowledging, not just with our lips but with our lives as well, that His ways are higher and better than our ways (Isaiah 55:8)—and that His plan, though infinitely greater than we can fathom, is for our good (Romans 8:28).

Living Open-Handedly

Let's talk about what it means to live your life open handed. It's simple. Imagine you hold out your hand, palm up, hand flat, and all that you have in this world is sitting in the palm of your hand. Meaning, you are not holding onto *anything* tightly or selfishly. Your hand is open, willingly releasing all you have. That is godly living. That is open-handed. But the minute we become like a toddler, the minute we let selfishness creep in, the minute we say the word *mine,* we move toward becoming unhealthy. If we try to close our hand around all of "our" things—if we try to say, "Well I earned it! I worked for it! I should be able to spend it the way I want!"— we are claiming ownership that we do not have and are moving toward an unhealthy lifestyle.

This is because we are acting out of pride instead of humility. We are exalting ourselves instead of God. It is a selfish perspective to believe that any gain we have is a result of our own worth or merit instead of understanding that "every good and perfect gift is from above" (James 1:17). When we ask if we are living with our hands open or closed, it is a deeper question of the heart. It's the question, "When God asks, how will I respond?"

God called Jonah to go and prophesy to the people of Nineveh (Jonah 1). Jonah didn't like the instructions God gave him because he looked down on the evil people of Nineveh. So he ran. Anyone who has ever tried to run from God knows it just doesn't work. Eventually, God snagged him, but not until he'd been thrown overboard in the middle of a horrible storm at sea and swallowed by an enormous fish (Jonah 1:17).

We are often tempted to read this story with a hint of pride and think, "Oh, that guy Jonah. He should have known better." But are we that different, really? Have there not been times when God asked each of us to go and meet a neighbor, give up some free time to do something we didn't want to do, or give some money we had earmarked for a vacation (or a new grill, or some new shoes) to the church, and we dug in our heels and refused? Let's be honest about it.

God will get what He needs from us in the end. The difference is whether we are holding His gifts in our open hands, where He can easily take them, or clutching them tightly, refusing to let them go. We are called to give cheerfully—to trust that if God asks something of us, it is in our best interest. He's calling you to help with Sunday school. Will you begrudgingly fill in only when necessary and with much complaining? Or will you make the most of the opportunity to serve?

A healthy follower of Christ and a healthy church realize that everything they have comes from God and is His do with as He pleases. When God asks something, they respond with, "Thank You, God, for all You have given me. Here it is—it's Yours." An unhealthy church says, "Thanks, God, but please don't take anything more than what I've set aside for You."

People often ask me how much they should give. I think that's really between an individual and God. When it comes to money, a good place to start is to tithe ten percent of your income. However, God might ask you for more, or you might not yet be able to give that much and have to start with less. You should be giving enough that you feel it—that it's a sacrifice—no matter what it is that you're being called to give. A wise man once said to me that you should give enough, whatever that amount is, to let God know that at any time, He can have the rest.

Generosity Versus Legalism

I have experienced a lot of closed-handed churches. The people come in, and everything is about what they get from the service. Their attitude says, "The sermon must be just so, the music like this, my pew for my family only, and my child treated this way. Everything in life exists for my pleasure and my comfort. I will set aside this amount and give it, but not a penny more, not an extra minute— not at the expense of my comfort."

In Matthew 23, Jesus is confronting the Pharisees head-on for being legalistic about several things, including their giving. The Pharisees took great pleasure in following the letter of the law, but their hearts were untouched by God's goodness. In verse 23, Jesus points out that the Pharisees even give ten percent of their spices. Imagine buying a bag of paprika, weighing it, measuring out a tenth, and taking it to the temple. Seems a bit silly, doesn't it? They were hyper-focused on the "tenth," but their hearts were wrong.

The real problem, Jesus said, was that the Pharisees gave what was easy but were stingy with justice, mercy, and faithfulness. They did the bare minimum and then checked "giving" off their to-do lists, continuing on their way, ignoring the hungry and hurting people around them. Jesus made it clear what He expects: "You should have practiced the latter, without neglecting the former." The King James Version says, "These ought ye to have done, and not to leave the other undone.

Do we have this issue? Do we pick and choose the things in the Bible, the things in church, the things in worship that we want to do, want to help with, want to give, and leave the other things for someone else?

Generosity is—at its simplest—a heart issue. There isn't a set amount of money that will force God to do what you want. God isn't manipulated that way. Giving your time won't make Him forgive your sins more completely or erase your guilt. We aren't to join the worship team so we can control what songs are played or have everyone recognize our talents.

We give cheerfully because Jesus gave everything for us. He gave up comfort in heaven to come to earth. He suffered horribly and bore the wrath of God for our sins. When we understand all that, our natural reaction should be, "What can I do for You, Father?" God's love for us was so great that He gave His Son for our sins, and we show Him our love by being open-handed with everything He's given us.

WORKBOOK

Chapter Nine Questions

Am I? What are your most prized possessions? These could be actual material items, as well as intangible treasures such as a career, a degree, family or friend relationships, or particular talents, skills, or hobbies. How would your actions and motives change if you saw yourself as a steward rather than the owner of each of these treasures? How can each of these be enjoyed and used for God's eternal purposes?

_____

_____

_____

_____

_____

_____

_____

_____

_____

_____

_____

Are We? In what ways is your church living generously within your community? How is your church giving to missionaries and their work? How is your church helping the poor, both locally and globally? Are you generous to families and individuals within the church who are in need? What are needs other than financial that your church focuses on meeting, such as counseling, refuge during a natural disaster, and safe family activities?

_____

_____

_____

_____

_____

_____

_____

_____

_____

_____

_____

Journal: Examine your heart when it comes to giving. Are you giving legalistically, trying to appease God, or giving generously, out of love for Him? Describe a time in your life when you gave out of sheer joy, perhaps to a loved one or to God. How can you capture that spirit in all of your giving?

_____

_____

_____

_____

_____

_____

_____

_____

_____

_____

_____

Action: Challenge yourself in the area of giving. What special need can you meet? What special need can your church work together to meet? (These could be financial or involve giving of your time/talents.) In what way can your giving be more sacrificial and personal instead of a line item in a budget or a distant online transaction?

Chapter Nine Notes

CHAPTER TEN

Missional Living

Then Jesus came to them and said, "All authority in heaven and on earth has been given to me. Therefore go and make disciples of all nations, baptizing them in the name of the Father and of the Son and of the Holy Spirit, and teaching them to obey everything I have commanded you. And surely I am with you always, to the very end of the age."
—Matthew 28:18–20

A healthy church is made up of people who, individually and collectively, answer Jesus' call to reach *all* people and bring them into the fullness of a loving, Christ-following community.

I love the church. The church is the bride of Christ! The world *needs* the church. But as the church, we have to re- member we are a community, not a building. We are many members of one body, not a social club. In order for us to fulfill our God-given purpose as the church, we have to swim upstream, to go against everything this world tries to compel us to become. We must grab hold of the

Scriptures and understand this truth: "greater is He who is in you than he who is in the world" (1 John 4:4 NASB). We must remember that "the Spirit God gave us does not make us timid, but gives us power, love and self-discipline" (2 Timothy 1:7).

The Single Biggest Problem

From the Bible, we know that Satan is the deceiver. We grow up knowing that the devil is the enemy of all Spirit-filled followers of Christ. I believe that the enemy is real. I believe that he works against us and against the causes of Christ. We absolutely must be aware and prepared to stand firm against him.

But here's the truth: the devil is *not* our biggest problem. Did you hear that? The greatest enemy to the cause of Christ and His church is not Satan. *It is us.* Yes, you and me. This is why, when Jesus said, "Whoever wants to be my disciple must...," He did not continue the sentence with "deny Satan." No, He didn't. He said, "Whoever wants to be my disciple must *deny themselves*" (Matthew 16:24, emphasis added).

God gave us a choice to love or not to love, and to serve or not to serve, which means we can choose selfishness. And since the time of Adam and Eve, and the fruit and the fall, man has been beyond selfish. We have to deny ourselves, our desires, our wants: "He must become greater; I must become less" (John 3:30).

Jesus is not afraid of, overwhelmed by, or even slightly concerned about the devil. He won the battle and overcame sin and death when He came the first time; He will overcome Satan when He comes the second time, too. Again, this means the single greatest obstacle to the church fulfilling our mission is us—the very people called to do missions.

Stop Playing Church Games

I used to wait tables at a couple of different popular chain restaurants. I honestly enjoyed those jobs. I enjoyed the people I worked with—they were nothing like me, and very few were believers, but I liked them. I was, however, truly saddened by what they saw and experienced from people "like me." Do you know that very few servers want to work Sundays? They detest working Sundays because they dread waiting on "church people." Unfortunately, they feel that way for a reason.

The church people we regularly experienced on Sundays were impatient and often rude, had incredibly high expectations yet showed very little gratitude, and were among the worst tippers in the industry—and not much has changed since I worked those jobs. That hurts my heart. We serve a loving, caring, gracious, and giving God. Yet the people who should see Jesus the most in us see us as completely the opposite. That's the kind of impression too many of us Christians are making on the rest of the world. And let's be clear, we have only ourselves to blame.

We like to experience church in comfortable seats in attractive buildings, with the words to the songs we like showing up on nice big screens. And if we don't like it, no problem—we can just pick another place.

"You won't sing hymns, so I will go somewhere else."

"You want drums, so I will go somewhere else."

"If I can't tell you where to spend the money, I will go somewhere I can."

Where in the Bible does Jesus say, "Pick another place"? Where does Scripture tell us that the church and its leadership should act and react to our personal preferences? In which book of the Bible does God say to switch churches whenever you want, and as often as you want, so that you are happy?

God told His people, "I reared children and brought them up, but they have rebelled against me" (Isaiah 1:2). And because they rebelled through disobedience, He told them, "Stop bringing meaningless offerings! Your incense is detestable to me. ... I cannot bear your worthless assemblies. .... When you spread out your hands in prayer, I hide my eyes from you" (Isaiah 1:13–15).

In other words, God is tired of us engaging in our same old weekly religious routines because we think they're the right thing to do—as we sacrifice to heaven on Sunday while living like hell the rest of the week. He's sick of His people raising their hands and singing songs to Him, because while we're praising Him with our lips, we're too often ignoring Him with our life. God doesn't want our superficially sacrificial, phony-religious selves. This is the essence of hypocrisy, and the world can't stand it. As it turns out, neither can God (see Revelation 3:14–22 and 1 John 4:20).

Then, the New Testament tells us, Jesus came down hard on God's people again:

You are like whitewashed tombs, which look beautiful on the outside but on the inside are full of the bones of the dead and everything unclean. In the same way, on the outside you appear to people as righteous but on the inside you are full of hypocrisy and wickedness.
—Matthew 23:27–28

"You're doing church things," Jesus told them, "but I want you to stop playing church games!" When God's people looked to Him and asked, "Where have You been? We've been fasting and sacrificing, just the way You commanded," He responded, in effect, "Where do you get the audacity to ask Me where I am? Where are your justice, mercy, and faithfulness? (Matthew 23:23, paraphrase). Why do you think you can pick and choose which good things you're going to do and then call yourselves 'good'?" This is what Jesus meant when He called out the people for straining out gnats while swallowing camels (Matthew 23:24).

We don't get to pick which parts of the Bible make us holy. Even if we focus all our energy on cleaning ourselves up on the outside, God still sees what's going on inside our hearts. As we saw earlier, since Adam and Eve first covered their nakedness in the Garden of Eden (Genesis 3:7), people have been trying to pull one over on God. Do we really think an omnipresent God can't see where you were and what you were up to? How much money you made last week versus how much you gave to your church or to those in need? God sees perfectly well when we're "whitewashed tombs," playing by the world's rules, and when His priorities are ruling in our hearts.

Eternal salvation isn't the end of our mission. We

celebrate bringing people into God's kingdom, and rightly so, but we're wrong to think that's the end, because ultimately the Bible and the gospel aren't about you or me— they're about God. We cannot simply evangelize and neglect discipleship. We must continue on in our journey after salvation and move towards restoration and reconciliation. This ultimately brings glory to God and God alone because only He can save and restore. It's *all* about God, who will bring *His* work in you to completion (Philippians 1:6).

The Commission Is the Mission

After Jesus died on the cross, rose again, and appeared to a number of people, He issued a final mandate to His followers to point them in the right direction:

> *All authority in heaven and on earth has been given to me. Therefore go and make disciples of all nations, baptizing them in the name of the Father and of the Son and of the Holy Spirit, and teaching them to obey everything I have commanded you. And surely I am with you always, to the very end of the age.*
> **—Matthew 28:18–20**

Three particular aspects of this Great Commission deserve a closer look: how godly authority works, what it means to "make disciples of all nations," and why our common understanding of baptism doesn't go deep enough.

Kingdom Authority

Please don't kill the child. I want the child. Please give me the child.[9]
—Mother Teresa, National Prayer Breakfast, 1997

Though Mother Teresa found abortion sinful and appalling, she didn't try to persuade, guilt, or shame anyone into agreement with her. Instead, she sought to disarm those who disagreed by humbling and giving of herself. In this, she demonstrated Jesus' style of authority.

When Jesus declared, "All authority in heaven and on earth has been given to me," the word He used for "authority" was *exousia*,[10] which encompasses the right to wield power, the power to exercise this right, and the area in which this power is exercised.[11] To His disciples, *exousia* likely brought to mind the regimented authority and strength of the Roman empire—an authority established by force, through swords and spears.

But Jesus spent His earthly life and ministry declaring and showing people a different kind of *exousia*: Kingdom power, or godly authority, one of the fruits of which is peace. He didn't come to fight those who opposed God—not in any conventional sense of fighting—but to disarm His opponents. Like Mother Teresa, who followed in His footsteps almost two thousand years later, He declined to enforce faith and righteousness at sword-point. He chose to love, serve, and draw people to Himself. He earned the authority instead of demanding the authority.

Since in Christ "we live and move and have our being"

(Acts 17:28), let's also follow Him by effecting spiritual authority through the way we live our lives, pouring honesty and integrity out into the world. Let's show the world we're willing to kneel and serve, even if it costs us our lives, so others may live, instead of trying to show the world how well we live. And let's take responsibility for personally answering Jesus' call to serve, instead of simply praying, passing the offering plate, and assuming His call was meant for someone else.

"All Nations" Means *All* People

Jesus called us to make disciples of *all* nations. The Greek word for *nations* is *ethnos,*[12] from where we get our word *ethnic,*[13] or *ethnicity.* Now, we tend to see *ethnos* as "across borders" or "other countries," but its simplest meaning is "people who are not like you." It means the ones you consider "others." The Great Commission does mean to go across borders, but it also means to go next door, down the street, or anywhere there are individuals who are "not like you" and are still in need of the gospel.

Many churches in America are full of people from the same socio-economic class. They have similarly priced homes and share the same skin color. There may be some legitimate demographic explanations for this reality, but ultimately, what does it say about how we're doing when it comes to the Great Commission?

The Great Commission isn't just about leading people to Christ who look like you, talk like you, live like you, and think like you. When Jesus spoke about all nations, He was talking about all people! This is including all ethnicities—including people who aren't anything like you.

Immersed in His Name

The word *baptizing* literally means to immerse.[14] It symbolizes dying with Jesus and being born again with Him, and is a testimony of what God has done in the believer's life. Baptism is the first sermon you can preach— without saying a word.

Jesus commanded His disciples to baptize "in the name of the Father and of the Son and of the Holy Spirit" (Matthew 28:19). When we do this, yes, we are very literally, verbally, following the Great Commission. However, spiritually, baptism also means to bring others into the community of God. As I mentioned in Chapter Six, God Himself is a community of three persons, who together are one God. So, the very personhood of God is community, and He wants us to immerse His disciples into His community.

The name of God is also important here. When you think about a name, it points to everything you are, your family, and the circumstances into which you were born. You can say a lot of things about me. I'm hyper, bald, short, and married to an incredibly beautiful woman! But this doesn't come close to covering everything about me. Craig Tackett is who I am, all of me. In the same way, we're baptizing people into all of who God is.

Sometimes we baptize people into the way we act in the world, too often in a spirit of hypocrisy (which is why they don't come). But we are to immerse them into what

God really is, along with all of the fruits of the Spirit. We aren't to immerse people into what we think God ought to be, but we must cover them in all that He truly is.

At a basic but critical level, you're already involved in missions. You are already involved in the Great Commission. The word we translate as *go* in Matthew 28:19 is not a tense we use in our English language. The Greek tense of the word encompasses the idea that you go "as you are currently going, and have been going, and continue to go."[15] Basically, this is telling us: in the middle of your going-ness, make disciples as you are, where you are—as you go!

People are seeing you, watching you, and deciding whether or not they want to be a part of the community you are a part of. And more importantly, whether they want anything to do with the God you claim to serve. We are to immerse every disciple we can find into the church family. It's not about rules, regulations, business, or money, but about Jesus, the fruits of the Spirit, and plugging people into the body of Christ to serve as they are gifted to serve. We want them to get actively involved in the community of God. This is when we'll be carrying out the Great Commission.

The Mission of a Healthy Church

If you choose to clap and cheer for Jesus, but do nothing more with your belief, that is absolutely your decision to make. Please realize that in the end, simply being a fan of God isn't going to amount to much. God is calling His disciples to get in the game! God is the Lord of the universe, and *He* deserves and demands much more from us than our applause.

Go and *do*. Volunteer your time, your energy, and your resources. You can start this with your next-door neighbor, with the kid alone in the lunchroom at school, or at the Salvation Army across the street. If no missionaries are coming out of your church, this is unhealthy. Healthy churches send people out. Healthy churches make disciples. Perhaps one of the reasons churches aren't sending more missionaries is because children aren't seeing the adults in their churches living out what God's calling them to do.

Covered in His Dust

What does it mean to make disciples? You can't follow the Great Commission if you don't even know what Jesus was asking you to make. The word for *disciple* is suggestive of being a student.[16] Disciples are to be students of Jesus, becoming more like Him.

In the Old Testament, a student chose a rabbi and became his disciple. It is a lot like how we choose a denomination or a church family today. Each rabbi had a different set of beliefs and interpretations when it came to Scripture. So a student would listen to the rabbis' teachings and decide who he wanted to follow, be like, and learn from.

A customary greeting at the time was, "May the dust of your rabbi cover you."[17] As the rabbi and students walked from town to town, their sandals would kick up dust. The person walking closest to the rabbi, following in his footsteps, would be covered in his dust. This was the place of honor, right behind the rabbi. You aren't to lead or command, but to follow your Rabbi! We should follow Jesus with the innocence and adoration of a little child following his father through a deep snowfall, jumping happily from one footstep to the next.

Let's create a culture of people who learn that their only goal is to be one step behind Jesus. Sometimes, we expect Jesus to walk beside us and be our friend. We think He wants our opinion about what to do with His money and His book. But the way it works is that He tells us what to do—and we follow. That's discipleship. Discipleship can be seen in the essence of the two-word invitation Jesus gave to his original disciples: "Follow Me."

God's Promise

"What if I fail?"
You will.
"What if I can't speak?"
Your life will.

The last promise Jesus made was this: "I will be with you." He didn't promise us that we'd get the girl, pass the course, preserve our marriage, or avoid the death of a loved one. However, He promised simply that through it all, He would be with us.

If we follow the Great Commission, will our church grow? I don't know! If you start tithing, will you be able to afford a bigger house? I don't know! If you start evangelizing, will God cure your momma's cancer? I don't know! Anyone who says they know is not being honest with you.

Jesus promised to be with you. If you're poor, sick, or otherwise in need, He will be with you. We just have to make a decision. Is that enough? Are you satisfied with the presence of God in your life? If everything else is taken away, would Jesus be sufficient?

You will have life and have it to the fullest (John 10:10) if you are one step behind Jesus. This is how we move toward a healthier church. And this is how He *changes the world* through us.

Chapter Ten Questions

Am I? In what ways are you taking it as your personal responsibility to reach people for God? In what ways might you be avoiding this commission as a personal responsibility? How, specifically, can you better reach people who are not demographically similar to you?

_____

_____

_____

_____

_____

_____

_____

_____

Are We? As a church, how are you doing in our calling to reach *all* people for Christ? In what ways are you going beyond water baptism, rules, and regulations, to immerse new believers and members in Jesus-focused, biblical community? How could your church do better in these respects?

_____

_____

_____

_____

_____

_____

_____

_____

_____

_____

Journal: To what extent are you going through the motions of a spiritual life instead of purposefully following Jesus? In what aspects of your life are you "climbing"— trying to succeed in earthly terms? Where in your life do you need to grow closer to God by kneeling to His instructions and purposes?

_____

_____

_____

_____

_____

_____

_____

_____

_____

_____

_____

Action: In prayer and as you read His Word, ask God what He wants you to give of yourself and your resources for Him—including to those in need. Now, go and *do* it!

Chapter Ten Notes

CONCLUSION

Am I?

Here's what I would like for you to do: as we end, I want to ask yourself, "Am I?" for every one of these. Here we go:

- Am I a person who believes that the Scriptures are sufficient?

- Am I pursuing Jesus?

- Am I a person who obeys the ordinances of Christ?

- Am I open-handed with all that He has given me?

- Am I willing to engage and be engaged by the people in this body?

- Am I chasing holiness?

- Am I celebrating the freedom that I have in Jesus Christ?

- Am I able to earnestly *repent* from the sins that I know I have, instead of just saying them out loud?

- Am I willing to be disciplined and to learn, along with the pastor, how to discipline discerningly within the body?

I don't want to be "that guy"; I want to be *His* guy. I want that for you also. I know that some of you are toeing the line. I know that you know it, too. I know that some of you are playing Christian, and you know it as well.

Some of you are dancing within the lines of your freedom and all you care about is the I's and the me's. If that's you, then it's time to put your hands up, lay your issues down, and slowly walk away from that life and toward something infinitely better. It's time to be honest with yourself. What are you struggling with right now? What do you truly want to do with your life? Do you want to make an eternal difference?

Your church's health depends on your health. Your health depends on your church's health. Let's be a healthy church together.

REFERENCES

Notes

1. McMillan, Greg. "6 Key Factors to Achieving Your Marathon Goal." Podium Runner. 2018. https://www.podium runner.com/training/marathon-training/6-key-factors-to-achie ving-your-marathon-goal/.

2. U.S. Department of Health and Human Services. "CDC National Health Reports Highlights." 2014. https:// www.cdc.gov/healthreport/previous/2014/publications/Compe ndium.pdf.

3. Eckel, Robert H., and Ronald M. Krauss. "American Heart Association Call to Action: Obesity As a Major Risk Factor for Coronary Heart Disease." 1998. https://doi.org/10.1161/ 01.CIR.97.21.2099.

4. *Blue Letter Bible,* "Strong's H259 – 'echad." https://www. blueletterbible.org/lang/lexicon/lexicon.cfm?Strongs=H259&t =KJV.

5. *Blue Letter Bible,* "Strong's H259 – 'echad."

6. Tozer, A. W. *The Pursuit of God.* Christian Publications, 1948, p. 63.

7. *Blue Letter Bible,* "Strong's G2431 – *hilaros.*" https://www.blueletterbible.org/lang/lexicon/lexicon.cfm?Strongs=G2431&t=KJV.

8. *Lexico,* "hilarious." https://www.lexico.com/definition/hilarious.

9. Peck, Bethany. "Canonizing Mother Teresa for Her Exaltation of Life." March for Life, 2016. https://marchforlife.org/jeanne-mancini-op-ed-washington-times/.

10. *Blue Letter Bible,* "Strong's G1849 – *exousia.*" https://www.blueletterbible.org/lang/lexicon/lexicon.cfm?Strongs=G1849&t=KJV.

11. *Baker's Evangelical Dictionary of Biblical Theology,* "authority." In Bible Study Tools. https://www.biblestudytools.com/dictionary/authority/.

12. *Blue Letter Bible,* "Strong's G1484 – *ethnos.*" https://www.blueletterbible.org/lang/lexicon/lexicon.cfm?Strongs=G1484&t=KJV.

13. *Lexico,* "ethnic." https://www.lexico.com/definition/ethnic.

14. *Blue Letter Bible,* "Strong's G907 – *baptizō.*" https://www.blueletterbible.org/lang/lexicon/lexicon.cfm?Strongs=G907&t=NIV.

15. *Bible Hub,* "4198. poreuomai." https://biblehub.com/greek/4198.htm.

16. *Blue Letter Bible,* "Strong's G3100 – *mathēteuō.*" https://www.blueletterbible.org/lang/lexicon/lexicon.cfm?Strongs=G3100&t=NIV.

17 Tverberg, Lois. "Covered in the Dust of Your Rabbi: An Urban Legend?" 2012. https://ourrabbijesus.com/covered-in-the-dust-of-your-rabbi-an-urban-legend/.

About the Author

Craig Tackett lives in Nicholasville, KY, with his incredible wife Jamie and three children—Tyler, Taycin, and Caton. He has been in the ministry for nearly thirty years and is currently serving as the pastor of NBC On Main.